Football Coach's Complete Scouting
and Game-Plan Guide

**Also by the Author**

*The Multiple Secondary System for Winning Football*

*Football's New Multiple Defense*

# FOOTBALL COACH'S COMPLETE SCOUTING AND GAME-PLAN GUIDE

Bobby Rexrode

Parker Publishing Company, Inc.          West Nyack, New York

© 1983, by

PARKER PUBLISHING COMPANY, INC.

West Nyack, N.Y.

**Library of Congress Cataloging in Publication Data**

Rexrode, Bobby.
  Football coach's complete scouting and game-plan
guide.

  Includes index.
  1. Football—Scouting.  2. Football—Coaching.
I.  Title.
GV953.4.R48  1983      796.332'2      83-4055
ISBN 0-13-324038-X

Printed in the United States of America

## DEDICATION

This book is dedicated to the following men, who made coaching the secondary so enjoyable for so many years: Jimmy Turner, Randy Wessinger, Gary Lowell, Eddie Wright, Grey Stogner, Chris Rockins and Raymond Polk.

## ACKNOWLEDGMENTS

This book would not have been possible without the help of the following coaches: Jerry Shaffer, Tommy Hudspeth, Larry Kramer, Jerry Cantrell, James Cameron, Dick String-fellow, Gerald Jack, Bill Lynch, David Nixon, Clovis Riley and John Groom. These men provided many of the ideas and a large number of the forms and charts contained herein.

My thanks also goes to Ray Overton, my high school coach, who was my inspiration for entering the coaching profession, and to Lynda and Gena for their help in preparing this material.

# HOW THIS BOOK WILL HELP YOUR GAME
# PREPARATION

"A good scouting job is worth 13 points to a team in any game," former Ohio State assistant coach, Esco Sarkkinen once said. Without a doubt, this statement is truer today than when it was made. The modern multiple offensive and defensive packages make a thoroughly organized scout report, transferred into a well-prepared game plan, worth between 17 and 20 points in any given game. With these thoughts in mind, the *Football Coach's Complete Scouting and Game-Plan Guide* was conceived.

Thoughtfully and carefully developed, the Complete Scouting and Game-Plan Guide will show you how to gain and use the information necessary to cope with the sophisticated offensive maneuvers of multiple motion, shifting, and other forms of formation distortion and the various spread formations; the defensive stunting, slanting, offsetting, stemming and multiple coverages which are so prevalent today.

The Scouting and Game-Plan Guide is designed for any size coaching staff. It has features that are especially prepared for a full staff which uses highly technical scouting techniques, including computerized methods. Conversely, the Guide provides an equal amount of valuable information for medium-size and small staffs, right down to the one-man staff whose student manager is the principal scout.

The thoroughness of your scout report/game plan system will be directly proportionate to the preparedness of your team each time you take the field, and the scoreboard will be the judge of how well your staff has prepared. Very often, too much time is directed toward the on-field practice of techniques, while too little time is spent in regard to how these techniques can affect the outcome of the next game.

With the Guide, you can properly prepare for each opponent with the confidence that you have turned over every stone in getting your staff and your players ready. The Guide presents you with a well-organized scouting system which, when combined with film study and the Guide's game plan preparation technique, will give maximum amount of pertinent information to your players for actual on-field preparation. This thorough type of preparation is worth two to five victories each season, according to the caliber of opposition played. Any less amount of scouting/game plan preparedness may well cost your team as many victories each year.

For the Head Coach, the Guide thoroughly outlines, explains and describes in depth the off-season, pre-season and in-season scouting organization; scout training techniques; organization of scouting materials; compilation and transfer of information to staff and team; preparation of game plan; and a well-organized plan for preparation of on-field workouts. Can you answer the question, "How Can We Win?" with confidence about each opponent with your present preparation system? If not, let the Guide help you reorganize your scouting/ game plan preparation system.

For the Offensive Coordinator, the Guide will show how to condition the scouting coach to bring back the specific information you need. Have you determined the tendencies of your next opponents in every possible way? Do you definitely know who are the weakest and who are the strongest members of the opponent's defensive front, linebackers and secondary? When you have your present game plan in hand, can you accurately answer the question "Where Can We Move It?" The Guide will help you answer this and many other important game preparation questions.

For the Defensive Coordinator, the Guide gives complete information on tendency-gathering methods, so you can show the scouting coach exactly what you want and how you want it. Can you presently set your defensive unit in an alignment and be completely confident that they are aligned to stop what your opponents do best? Are you sure when you go into each game that you have correctly answered the question, "What Must We Stop?" The Guide will help you prepare successfully for your opponent's best, in 1, 2, 3 order.

For the Coach who scouts, whether you are a beginner or a veteran, the Guide contains from A to Z the materials, scouting techniques, compilation techniques and transition and information transfer techniques which will help you help your team prepare to be a winner. Special features also tell you how to pick up tip-offs and other important "sideline information" which is so essential in defeating opponents who are equal in capability. Let the Guide help make you an even more invaluable asset to your football program.

Regardless of your station on the coaching staff, let the *Football Coach's Complete Scouting and Game-Plan Guide* provide you with the information you need to be well prepared every time you play. Remember, it all boils down to: "Where Can We Move It?" "What Must We Stop?" "How Can We Win?"

*Bobby Rexrode*

# TABLE OF CONTENTS

# 1

# HOW CAN WE WIN?
## (Head Coach)

How Can We Win? This is undoubtedly the single most important question a Head Coach can ask before and during his staff's game-plan preparation for the next opponent. The purpose of this chapter is to help the Head Coach be sure he has left no stone unturned in finding the answer to "How Can We Win?" As you will see, this chapter deals only with the early portion of the game preparation period for a weekend to aid the Head Coach in outlining and organizing his game planning activity. As is usually the case, neither this chapter nor this book can provide everything for everyone in game-plan preparation. The purpose of both this chapter and this book is to provide some new and different thoughts and confirm some time-honored beliefs in the realm of the Scout Report/Game Plan transition, and combine the two into a stronger game-planning system for your program.

The question, "How Can We Win?" should be asked several times by the Head Coach and his Assistant Coaches during game-plan preparation. The Head Coach, for example, should ask the question of each Scout, each Assistant Coach, and finally himself, after all the facts are in about the next opponent and before actual game-plan preparation goes on paper.

Too many times, however, "How Can We Win?" gets overlooked and lost in the shuffle during the feverish and hectic staff preparation period for the next opponent. A day or a day and a half is a very short time to be completely thorough in preparing a game plan. This becomes truer each day that passes. In this era of highly technical football, featuring complicated, multi-faceted offenses and defenses, game planning in the proper manner is just too important to leave anything to chance.

In order to be sure there is time to ask and answer the question, "How Can We Win?" the Head Coach must carefully organize his staff's game-plan preparation time each week. He must be especially careful to allot himself the necessary time (half a day) to prepare a sound, concise and solid answer to "How Can We Win?" Why do I continue to repeat this phrase? Because if you do not answer it correctly, many times all the work you, your staff and your team do, will go right down the drain. Proper organization of game-plan preparation will assure the Head Coach that outside interference and other distractions will not stand in the way of answering the most important question of all.

Proof that the question, "How Can We Win?" often gets overlooked can easily be seen through the following example: Have you ever played a team inferior to yours and thought you were well prepared, only to find your team being dominated by the lesser group of youngsters? You know you should be winning, you believe you eventually will, but you cannot imagine what has happened to your team.

We have all been in that situation at least once. What is the cause? We often blame a poor game on one of several time-worn bugaboos, when the real truth is that the team was not properly prepared by the coaching staff! Oh, sure, we like to pass the buck with the old, "We were just flat" excuse. Actually, the coaching staff did not include the proper ingredients (whether physical or mental) in the game plan. This usually happens when the Head Coach fails to make himself and his staff find the answer to "How Can We Win?" before the actual game plan is finalized. When a staff makes sure this question is answered, it shows directly through to the team: (1) in the Scout Report; (2) in the Game Plan; (3) in the on-field practice sessions; and most important, (4) in the attitude of the coaching staff. Conversely, when "How Can We Win?" goes unanswered in game-plan preparation, the players can sense it

immediately; thus, their sometimes lackadaisical perform-
ances. Many times the caliber of an opponent, though it
should not, causes a staff to be either over-confident or
defeatist in attitude in preparing for that opponent. It should
be remembered that the attitude of the coaches will be the
attitude of the team. You cannot fool them.

I am sure you can think of a top-notch, winning team that
seems to play basically the same, week after week. They win
the close ones, score late to pull it out, and yet never appear to
be all that good physically. The secret is that the team's
coaching staff is totally organized in its preparation and, as a
result, so is the team—every week. When a staff prepares with
a common purpose, knows how it plans to win and shows the
enthusiasm of togetherness, the players pick up the positive
flow and react accordingly, regardless of the caliber of the
opponent. Remember, answer the question "How Can We
Win?" first, then the other things will begin to fall into place.

## GAME-PLAN PREPARATION

The remainder of this chapter will be devoted to providing an organizational plan for the early part of the staff's
preparation period. Keep in mind that this section is simply
meant to reinforce the need to put "How Can We Win?" in its
proper perspective.

The first thing the Head Coach must do, regardless of staff
size, is to get his game-plan preparation period completely
organized. There is an old saying, "If you fail to plan, you plan
to fail." This is no truer anywhere else than in organizing
game-plan preparation. Following are three very important
factors which must be dealt with first in planning the game-
plan preparation weekend.

### Always Be Positive

The most important thing you can do as a Head Coach, in
working with your staff, is to be positive. This is particularly
true during game-plan preparation. A coaching staff's week is
full of activity which may include:

1. A long week of teaching (in most cases);
2. Conducting workouts;
3. Game after game pressure;
4. Game plan preparation on the weekend.

The wise Head Coach will handle the game-plan preparation period very positively. By doing so, his staff will have a positive outlook and get more quality work done. Some things the Head Coach can do to start the game-planning period on a positive note are:

1. Pick up the game film yourself.
2. Provide hot coffee or cold drinks for the staff.
3. Provide doughnuts or hot rolls for the staff.
4. Find a time, preferably early, to compliment each coach on a job well done in the previous night's game. (Pick out something in particular which you can brag about him for, even if his group was terrible in general.)
5. Watch last night's film together as a staff. Coaches responsible for particular groups should grade their groups. Everyone enters into free discussion of all phases of the game. (This is good therapy.)
6. Hold a very short, easy-going, non-structured session in which each coach can unwind and feel free to say anything he wishes. After a few minutes (ten at most), tell a joke or two (clean, of course) and say, "O.K. men, let's go get ready to whip (*next opponent* )."
7. Make sure each Assistant Coach is scheduled for a particular phase of preparation.
8. Go to work yourself immediately on your game preparation.

## Remove All Interference and Distractions

When organizing game-plan preparation, the Head Coach should see that the field house or office is secure against all outside interference. Among the things you must do are:

1. Take the telephone off the hook; or
2. Have the student manager answer the telephone. Have him take messages. Check with him periodically to monitor any important calls. (This practice will do away with all those calls from reporters, well-wishers, gripers, salesmen and others. As Head Coach you must talk with these people and

cooperate with them when possible, but you must do so at a
time convenient to yourself. This is especially true when it
comes to game-plan preparation. Straight-through con-
centration for prescribed periods of time is very important
and demands the highest priority.)

3. Print Saturday's agenda for film viewing, game-plan preparation and the loosening-up workout, and see that each player
and parent gets a copy. Parents should be welcome at every
workout, including your Saturday loosening-up workout.
However, parents and game planning do not go together. You
should simply ask the players to reinforce the importance of
the game-planning period to their parents and ask them to
have their parents adhere to the printed schedule. By han-
dling it in this manner, the coaches will have their privacy
and the parents will realize they are helping your program by
cooperating. An example of a Saturday morning general
game-planning schedule can be seen in Figure 1-1, on page
28.

4. Players should leave the field house or office area immediately after viewing the previous night's film, going through
the loosening workout and taking care of any injuries. Time
away from the field house will be refreshing for the players
and will allow the coaches to fully concentrate on game
planning. During the week, the players are welcome and
encouraged to stay as late as they wish after workouts to view
films, go over the scout report or weight train.

## Use a Tape Recorder

How many times have you told your Scouts, "Never trust
anything to memory, record it immediately"? This is a good
idea for the Head Coach and the entire staff to remember. To
assure proper retention of information, every Head Coach (and
each Assistant, if possible) should have a tape recording
device. A tape recorder is especially helpful during the game-
plan preparation period. Among other things, the tape recorder may be used for:

1. Conversations with your Scouts;
2. Recording telephone calls to other coaches whose teams have
played upcoming opponents (very valuable information);
3. Your own descriptions of the next opponents as you view
film;

4. Discussions with your Assistant Coaches (particularly the Offensive and Defensive Coordinators);
5. Your own thoughts, as they develop, about the game plan.
6. You can listen to portions of the tape any time you have a few minutes. Then in the evening, you can run the entire tape through. This is a tremendous help when you begin to formulate the game plan with the Offensive and Defensive Coordinators. (It also keeps things organized for that ultimate question, "How Can We Win?")
7. Do not stop taking notes and making diagrams. The tape recorder is only a supplement. It will never replace the old X's and O's.

## HEAD COACH'S SCHEDULE

Size of staff will determine how independent the Head Coach can be in game-plan preparation. He should have some time by himself, regardless of staff size, to mull over possibilities. If he coaches one of the groups, such as the offensive backs, etc., he may spend some time in the grading process or film viewing with his group. He must remember, however, that this time should be abbreviated, for the next opponent looms large on the horizon. The next few pages will be devoted to an ideal tentative schedule of time division for the Head Coach during game-plan preparation. The amount of independent time the Head Coach has, again, will depend upon staff size.

### Obtain Scouts' Opinions

The first discussion session the Head Coach should have is with the Scouts who saw your next opponent play the previous night. With tape recorder running for memory retention, the Head Coach should ask questions of the Scouts that follow this outline:

1. Results of last night's game—score, the opponent's strength, weather, etc.;
2. Anything outstanding or unusual—offense, defense, kicking, returns;
3. Personnel—best, worst, new, injured, surprises;
4. Team strengths and weaknesses;

5. Anything else the Scouts want to add;
6. Ask, "How Can We Win?" The Scouts' opinions are usually valid. They have seen the opponents play in person. In most cases, no one on the Varsity staff has.

After this brief discussion, the Scouts should go back and continue the compiling of information and the Head Coach will prepare to view the opponent's film. If opponent's film is not available, go over last year's Scout Report/Game Plan, Post-Game Report, Off-Season and Pre-Season Reports.

## View Opponent's Film

If film trades are common in your area, you will probably have at least two films to view. If you do not trade, secure films by telephone earlier from coaches who have previously played your upcoming opponent. A good checklist to use in viewing films of your next opponent will include the following things:

1. Tape record your comments.
2. Take notes and diagram anything outstanding (both good and bad) and anything unusual team-wise.
3. Pay particular attention, and note and record numbers and names of the best and worst personnel, their positions and their particular strengths and weaknesses.
4. Check distance of kicks, depth of kickers and punters, and record.
5. Check the quickness of kickers and punters and passer's release.
6. Compare, in your mind, your team with theirs—offensively, defensively, kicking game and personnel-wise.
7. Call other coaches who have already played or scrimmaged your next opponent for their ideas and suggestions. Do this while the film is fresh in your mind. (Be sure to tape conversation.)
8. Record your thoughts at this time as to a very general, open-minded and basic answer to, "How Can We Win?"

## Consult the Offensive Coordinator

By this time, the Offensive Coordinator's schedule should be such that he can have a short talk with you. This discussion will entail the basic offensive theme which should now be developing. With the available prior knowledge about the opponent, the general thoughts of the Scouts, the Offensive Coordinator's thoughts and the Head Coach's ideas, a general pattern for the beginning of an offensive game plan should be developing. The purpose for this meeting is exactly that—to get a general idea from which the offensive game plan will finally emerge. Just before you break up the meeting, ask the Offensive Coordinator, "How Can We Win Offensively?" His answer at this point will likely be general, but it may be very important. (First impressions are correct at least 90% of the time.) Be sure to record this session.

This is a good place to make a very important point. In every discussion with Assistant coaches, you, as the Head Coach, must remember to keep a very open mind. Very often your Assistants come up with excellent ideas which may not match yours, at first. Before you disagree with an Assistant's proposal (aloud or to yourself), you should carefully think it over. He could be right.

## Consult the Defensive Coordinator

The Head Coach should talk with the Defensive coordinator immediately after the session with the Offensive Coordinator. This discussion should be very much like the one with the Offensive Coordinator. Simply have a short talk to get the drift of the Defensive Coordinator's ideas as compared to yours on the possible early direction of the defensive game plan. At the end of the conversation, ask him, "How Can We Win Defensively?" It is good to ask the Coordinators this question for two reasons: (1) their answers are usually valid and valuable; and, (2) it keeps their thoughts running along the same lines as yours with respect to answering that very important question.

## Head Coach's Analysis

Now you, the Head Coach, should be alone with the tape recorder, notes and diagrams. Lean back, relax, and listen to the tapes that have been collected all morning, while looking through and adding to your notes and diagrams. Pay particular attention to references to personnel, offense, defense and anything special which may come up. Remember that the single most important goal of the entire morning is to finally answer correctly the question, "How Can We Win?" When you complete the self-review period, ask yourself this question. By this time, the answer should at least be in the formative stage. By the process described in the last few pages, you will have arrived at the answer scientifically. This is most important, because many times haughtiness and an inflated ego after a big win the night before, or that sick feeling after a bitter loss can affect game planning. When the previously described schedule and methods are followed, however, every minute is occupied with the next opponent. This gets the staff's thoughts moving into the future which can, to some degree, be controlled. You surely cannot control the past, so why worry about it?

## Full Staff Meeting with Scouts

When the Scouts have compiled the pertinent information, the entire staff should meet with them and follow a procedure similar to the following guidelines.

1. Scouts deliver all basic Scout Report information and give their personal views on the opponents.
2. The Head Coach asks any personnel questions he has.
3. The Head Coach asks questions about the kicking game.
4. The Offensive Coordinator asks questions concerning the next opponent's defense.
5. The Defensive Coordinator asks questions concerning the next opponent's offense.
6. The Head Coach again asks each Scout and Varsity Coach individually, "How Can We Win?"
7. Remember to keep the tape recorder going during this session. In fact, all staff members can benefit greatly by having their morning's work recorded for later reference. It is a great help to flip on the tape player each evening and refresh your memory of all the important information. Information reinforcement is a very important phase of being completely prepared. The tape recorder is the simplest method of carrying out this reinforcement.

## ASSISTANT COACHES' SCHEDULES

Size of staff will again determine how much work the Assistant Coaches can get done in the Saturday morning period. The schedule that follows will be outlined for a full staff so that all facets are covered. If your staff is limited in numbers, the duties will have to be doubled up, but all should be covered.

1. Grade film (during staff meeting).
2. Short staff "free" session.
3. Meet players, discuss grades, view film of last night's game in groups (offensive, defensive, backs, line, etc.).
4. Conduct short loosening workout for team.
5. If needed, help treat injured players.
6. Check briefly with Scouts on Assistant Coach's specialty (tape recorder).
7. View film of next opponents (notes, diagrams and tape recorder).
8. Consult with Head Coach in pre-planning session about formation of preparation ideas (tape recorder).
9. Staff meeting with Scouts for information transfer (tape recorder). (See Figure 1-2 on page 29 for complete sample of Scout Report/Game Plan weekend organization.)

## LIMITED STAFF ORGANIZATION

A staff that is limited to one to three coaches will approach the game-plan preparation period somewhat differently than will the medium- or full-size staff. The important thing to remember in organizing the limited staff for game-plan preparation is: (1) keep it simple; (2) cover the necessary categories; and, (3) answer the question, "How Can We Win?" Actually, the major difference between the full and limited staffs is that on the limited staff, coaches have to double up on responsibilities.

Often, on very small staffs the only information available about the next opponent will be one film or an abbreviated scout report collected by an inexperienced coach or even the

Student Manager. In such cases, preparation methods and organization are even more important. Regardless of the size of the staff, the Head Coach must keep in mind the following points:

1. Be completely organized. (This is the first step on the ladder to victory.)
2. Stay as close to the previously listed schedule as possible. Double up where necessary. Usually, a smaller staff has fewer athletes. Therefore, many of the group meetings can be combined under the leadership of fewer coaches. This frees the others to begin game-plan preparation for the next opponents.
3. At all costs, remove all interference.
4. Use the tape recorder.
5. Be proud of your staff and your program. No matter what the size of your staff or your program, it is worthwhile. You are doing a good deed for many young people, and your work is very important to the community!

## BREAK

At this point (1:00 to 2:00 p.m., Saturday), everyone on the staff will be exhausted, both physically and mentally. I strongly believe the staff should take a long break at this time. A fatigued mind will not produce many successful plans and ideas. Breaking at this point has several positive aspects and allows the staff to go home and

1. Relax (watch college game on television, etc.);
2. Be with their families for a while;
3. Alternate films (see Figure 1-2) for reviewing;
4. Give further, more relaxed thought to possibilities for the game plan (use tape recorded material);
5. Form new ideas. Some of the best game-plan ideas come when one has relaxed for a while, had some time with his family, and cleared his mind. Then when he returns his thoughts to football, his mind turns out new and better ideas (like, "How Can We Win?").

## WRAP-UP

Game planning will resume at 1:00 p.m. on Sunday. I thoroughly believe this is better than trying to squeeze the entire transition from the previous night's game to completed preparation for next week's game into one day. Too much hurry, too much overlooked, too much at stake!

As was mentioned earlier, the purpose of this chapter is not to completely outline the game-plan preparation period, but to provide the Head Coach with some concrete ideas and

---

### SATURDAY PLANNING AND WORKOUT SCHEDULE

Bearcats and Parents,

As you know, the weekend is very short when it comes to getting over the bumps, bruises, big plays and excitement of the last game and beginning to prepare for the next game.

It is also a very short time for the coaching staff when preparing the game plan for our next opponents. With these facts in mind, please work with us on the following weekend schedule so that we all may be properly prepared for the next game.

*Saturday*

|  |  |
|---|---|
| 8:00 to 9:15 | Staff meeting |
| 9:15 to 10:15 | Players view film with staff and get grades |
| 10:15 to 10:45 | Loosening-up workout (parents welcome to watch workout) |
| 10:45 | Players off for weekend (unless injuries need treatment) |
| 10:45 to 1:00 | Game plan preparation for next opponent |

Please respect these hours unless there is an emergency. If so, please notify the person answering the telephone that it is an emergency. We will help in any way we can.

Thank you,

Bearcat Coaching Staff

---

Figure 1-1

checklists which will help keep priorities in line for proper organization which will help answer the most important question connected with any football game, "How Can We Win?"

Later, complete chapters are devoted to the game-plan preparation phases of Scout Report Information compilation, information transfer to the staff and preparing the game plan.

---

### SCOUT REPORT/GAME PLAN WEEKEND SCHEDULE

#### Saturday

| *Varsity Staff* | *Scouting Crew Compilation-(Non-Computer)* |
|---|---|
| 7:30- 8:00— *Head Coach* pick up game film | 7:30-12:00 |
| 8:00- 9:00— *Staff* grade film and discuss | 1. Complete card punch-out |
| 9:00- 9:15— Non-structured staff session | 2. Complete booklet totally |
| 9:15-10:15— *Head Coach*—begin game-plan preparation *Assistants*—show last night's film to players and discuss (2 projectors) (9:15-9:45 Off. line and Def. backs) (9:45-10:15 Def. line and Off. backs) | 3. Stack and tendency cards<br>4. Confirm by films<br>5. Color charts<br>6. All tendency charts<br>7. Personnel poster<br>8. Formations poster<br>9. Basic plays poster |
| 10:15-10:45— *Head Coach*—continue game-plan preparation *Assistants*—(1) Run team through short loosening workout (2) Begin game-plan preparation | |
| 10:45-12:00— *Everyone*—game-plan preparation | 12:00-1:00—Scouting Crew meet with Staff |
| 12:00- 1:00— *Staff* meet with Scouting Crew | |

*Break*

Films to Individual Coaches for Casual Viewing at Home

3:00-4:30—Coach #1
4:30-6:00—Coach #2
6:00-7:30—Coach #3      Alternate procedure weekly
7:30-9:00—Coach #4
9:00—to Head Coach (if necessary)

*Sunday*

1:30-2:30—Review opponent's films by Offensive-Defensive
            Coaches with Scouts
2:30-4:00—Complete game plan (offense, defense, kicking game)
4:00-4:30—Verify game plan and consider tentative Monday
            schedule

Figure 1-2

# 2

# WHERE CAN WE MOVE IT?
## (Offensive Coordinator)

Do NOT make your next opponents smarter than they actually are! How many times have you said, "If we try to do this, they will do that"? Are you sure? Often, coaches outsmart themselves when preparing an offensive game plan, because they give the upcoming opponents credit for having a "super mentality," which is usually not the case.

When this happens, the Offensive Coordinator often ends up: (1) limiting his attack too narrowly; (2) departing too much from his basic attack to concentrate on "fooling" the opponents with new offense and/or trick plays; or, (3) failing to identify the opponent's weaknesses and/or failing to properly direct the attack to the personnel or areas indicated. Far too much worry is often wasted on how the opponents will react, and not enough time is spent planning for their personnel and basic maneuvers.

In other words, a good thought for the Offensive Coordinator to keep in mind is: "I cannot control what they do, but I *can* control what we do, and we *will* do it well enough so that what they do will not matter." With these thoughts in mind, this chapter will provide the Offensive Coordinator with some sound principles concerning the scouting of and preparation for upcoming opponents' defenses. And finally, it will deal with answering the important question, "Where Can We Move It?"

## MAKE THE SCOUT REPORT MEANINGFUL

The first priority for the Offensive Coordinator, in preparing for an upcoming opponent, is to call for only the information he can use with respect to the scout report. Too often, scout report forms are used simply because another successful coach uses a similar type in his program, or for a variety of other unimportant reasons. Actually, most "form" scouting booklets are lacking in the area of defensive information required about an upcoming opponent.

To be sure that you (the Offensive Coordinator) get complete information concerning the upcoming opponent's defensive system, make the scouting material (booklet, forms, etc.) fit your specific needs. Keep in mind the following items when helping to develop the scouting materials:

1. Require information about the upcoming opponent's defensive scheme, according to your offensive philosophy.
2. Require information according to your personnel's strengths and weaknesses. (This may sometimes necessitate changing some of your forms from season to season, according to the type of personnel you have.)
3. Require specific information according to whether you depend more on the run or the pass.
4. Require specific information according to whether you depend more on speed and finesse than on power when running the football.
5. Require specific information according to what you like to do on critical downs in crucial situations.
6. Require specific information according to your type of goal-line and short-yardage offense, and your two-minute offense.
7. Require specific information concerning opponents' personnel strengths and weaknesses. (Those are hard to completely detect on film, particularly along the crowded line of scrimmage. Often, binoculars provide a much better view to the Scout on the spot.)
8. Require all the play-by-play information necessary to reveal any tendencies the opponents may exhibit. (Do not overdo this phase. Only get the information that can actually be used in formulating the game plan.)

Once the Offensive Coordinator has developed scouting forms that will deliver the proper information, he must then train the Scouts, who will collect the information. Actually, this phase of preparing for opponents may be the most important. A Scout who knows exactly what information the Offensive Coordinator wants, the best methods to obtain it, and how to present it, will be invaluable to game-plan preparation. Every minute spent helping Scouts learn their job will pay off at game-planning time.

## USE A ONE-STEP CAMERA

The possibilities of using a one-step rapid reproducing (still, single-photo) camera in the game-plan preparation process are unlimited. (Using this type of camera for scouting purposes is illegal in many states.) The one-step camera can be particularly useful in setting the opponent's basic alignments by snapping photos from the screen as film is being shown. A few practice shots is all a coach needs to be ready to add a new dimension to his preparation system. The uses of such a camera in planning are limited only by each coach's imagination.

To be able to have snapshots of the opponent's defensive alignments available at any time is a real plus for the Offensive Coordinator. It certainly saves a tremendous amount of ""at-home or in-class guesswork," while concentrating on the opponents during the week before the game. Give this inexpensive preparation method an opportunity to help your game planning. With a sound tape recorder and the one-step camera, the Offensive Coordinator can have two inexpensive, invaluable assets in planning for upcoming opponents.

## COMPILATION OF INFORMATION

Another very important area that the Offensive Coordinator must do a good job of teaching to the Scouts is the compilation of information about an opponent from the material in the scout report. Regardless of staff size, it is essential that the scouting information that is brought back be compiled together to produce the tendency factors needed by the Offensive Coordinator. Proper training in this area will insure that the Scouts have the capability to successfully carry out the correct compilation process. The Scouts should know how to deliver exactly what the Offensive Coordinator needs in order to determine the type of attack to employ in the game plan.

As to the compilation process itself, be sure to have compiled and charted only that information which will enhance your game plan. Any other information will only serve to split your attention and will eventually have to be sifted out anyway, so leave it out to begin with. Require the information to be compiled which will help you answer the question, "Where Can We Move It?" (Suggestions for the complete compilation process are found in Chapter 14.)

## ATTACKING OPPONENTS' STRENGTHS AND WEAKNESSES

Many times an Offensive Coordinator neglects a very integral part of planning for the attack of an opponent's defense. Attacking the strengths of a defense is often just as important as attacking its weaknesses. Whether the opponent's defensive strengths lie in the alignment used, their personnel, or in specific maneuvers; if these strengths are not systematically attacked (at least on occasion), they will flow and eventually prevent the successful attack of the opponent's weaknesses.

Take for example a very strong, quick, talented opposing defensive tackle. No matter how good he is, there is a way to be at least respectably successful in attacking him. (If he penetrates hard, trap, draw, screen or counter him, etc.) If he is not forced to stay at home, he will pursue quickly and cover up the weaknesses you are attempting to attack. (Besides, very often, defensive front players who appear awesome are better in pursuit than in defending their first responsibility. However, because of these players' reputations, few teams exploit all possibilities of attack.)

Another example may be a very tough strong safety who covers his flat area well and puts strong outside pressure on the run. An excellent way to attack the strong safety is to flood the strong side flat and deep ⅓, sprint out strong and block first contain. Now, no matter what the strong safety does, it will be wrong. These examples were given to prove that no matter how strong a defense is, it still must be attacked at its strongest points in order for its weak points to be open when it is crucial to attack them at critical points in the game.

Of course, all Offensive Coordinators are going to attack straight ahead and strongly any weaknesses a defensive opponent exhibits. Good rules of thumb for attacking strengths and weaknesses of defensive opponents are:

1. Scout the opponent accurately and thoroughly, pinpointing all defensive strengths and weaknesses.
2. Plan open-mindedly, fearing no opponent's ability nor being disrespectful of any opponent's lack of ability. (Fear none—respect all.)
3. Overload or decoy those opponents who have superior talents or other defensive strengths.
4. Go right at weaker players or other defensive flaws.
5. Keep a balance between attacking the strengths and weaknesses of the opponents to keep them honest. (Then, when it is critical, you can successfully attack their weaknesses!)
6. Know exactly what you want to do in 1, 2, 3, order when that crucial time comes in the game.
7. Remember, if you can challenge and defeat your opponent's strongest player early, it will have a terrifically demoralizing effect on the rest of their defensive players.

## WRAP-UP

This chapter was meant to give the Offensive Coordinator some positive points of reference in the preparation and use of the scouting materials in collecting information on opponents' defenses. Also, this chapter should prompt the Offensive Coordinator to help the Scout learn efficiency in the scouting and compilation processes, so that the Scout can provide the proper information in a valuable manner. Finally, the Offensive Coordinator should gain the confidence necessary in planning to attack the opponents on all levels, using the collected scouting information to pinpoint the type and intensity of offensive maneuvers to be used. All in all, the Offensive Coordinator must take each of these things into consideration in answering the question, "Where Can We Move It?"

# 3

# WHAT MUST WE STOP?
## (Defensive Coordinator)

INDIVIDUAL and team morale are the single most important factors in any defensive unit's success. Therefore, the Defensive Coordinator must completely investigate, correctly evaluate, and thoroughly plan for every opponent, so his players will have confidence in each game plan. When a defensive unit plays with a positive attitude, knowing basically what the opponents will do and when, the aggressiveness of that unit will be the difference in many close games. Suffice it to say then, that all other things being equal, the defensive team that has been prepared through the use of an accurate scout report and an effective game plan will most often successfully stop its opponents. The beginning of defensive success is a well-organized scout report on the upcoming opponent's offense, which will help the Defensive Coordinator decide, "What Must We Stop?"

## DETERMINE WHO, WHERE AND HOW

The first and most important items the Defensive Coordinator must be able to determine from the scout report are: (1) who are the opponent's best-skilled position players; (2) where do these skilled position players best attack the defense; and, (3) how (what methods used) does the offense attack these defensive areas?

To get the above-mentioned information thoroughly and accurately, the Defensive Coordinator must spend some time in the off-season and pre-season on training the Scouts in proper information-gathering procedures. Once the Scouts become proficient in the normal information-gathering process, the Defensive Coordinator should instruct them carefully in picking up various tip-offs. Tip-offs are very important to the defense in any game. In a game against an outstanding offense, taking advantage of tip-offs can often be the difference between victory and defeat. All in all, the Defensive Coordinator can spend a large portion of his off-season and pre-season time in no better way than to work with the Scouts in his system.

When the Scouts are capable of bringing back exactly what the Defensive Coordinator wants with respect to Who, Where and How, he then is in a postion to decide what he wants to take away from the opponent's offense and in what order. Before determining the order in which he wishes to take away offensive maneuvers, however, the scouting information should be compiled and tendencied by the Scouts. Then the game planning can begin.

## USE ALL AVAILABLE MATERIALS

The use of a tape recorder and a one-step camera in game planning has already been mentioned in Chapters 1 and 2. Both of these devices and other materials can also be used to great advantage in defensive game planning. One phase of the compilation process, for example, is the making of color charts to tendency formations, points of attack and ball carriers. (These are usually used in standard, non-computerized systems.) In filling out color charts, brightly colored marking pens can be utilized. Other uses of colored marking pens include:

1. Color coding play-by-play diagraming cards;
2. Opponent's formation posters (bulletin board);
3. Opponent's basic running and pass play posters (bulletin board);

4. Opponent's play cards (to be used by offensive scout team in workouts).

The use of bright colors in game preparation materials, particularly on posters for the team bulletin board, provides a positive atmosphere. Also, brightly colored posters will draw more continued attention from the players, and are just as easy to make as those made with plain black markers. Another positive aspect of using colors for posters is that outstanding individual opponents who are to be highly keyed can be pinpointed by a specific color each week. In addition to these suggestions, the staff should use any other materials available to "brighten up" the game-plan material which will adorn the field house or which will be handed out to the players.

## COMPILATION AND EVALUATION

Another thing that the Defensive Coordinator would be wise to teach in the off-season and pre-season is preparing the Scouts to properly compile information concerning offensive opponents. If the Scouts are competent in the proper compilation methods, the Defensive Coordinator will be in a position to evaluate the opponent's offense objectively. He can then make wise decisions as to what he wishes to take away from the opponents and in which order.

Once the Defensive Coordinator has the compiled information from the Scout report, he then must begin a very important decision-making evaluation process. In evaluating the opponent's offensive attack, the Defensive Coordinator must determine which are the most dangerous facets of the attack, and begin to decide how he will combat them. As the Defensive Coordinator is considering how he will approach stopping the opponents, he must evaluate the following general aspects of their attack:

1. Personnel (as a team and individually);
2. Style of offense;
3. Formations used;
4. Type of running game (power, option, finesse);

5. Type of passing game (drop back, play action, sprint);
6. Attack balance (strongside oriented, weakside oriented, or equal balance).

## TAKING AWAY THEIR BEST FIRST

After studying the compiled scouting information and film on the opponent's offense, and talking with the Head Coach and Scouting Crew, the Defensive Coordinator should begin to draft specific defensive maneuvers to stop the opponent's best plays and players. In this phase of game planning, it must be decided exactly what must be stopped in 1, 2, 3 order. While making these decisions, the Defensive Coordinator should focus the scope of his game plan directly on only the very best things the opponents do offensively.

The defensive game plan will likely follow one of the three basic time-honored schemes:

1. Normal (based on opponent's habit of using a balanced offensive attack);
2. Ram (based on opponent's habit of using an all-out power running offensive attack);
3. Aerial (based on opponent's habit of using the pass as the basic form of attack).

Of course, within each of the above schemes, adjustments will be necessary depending on the opponent's best maneuvers and personnel. For example, the game plan may be based on one of the following criteria:

1. Universal (defend the opponent's entire offense equally, putting no special emphasis on any particular phase. Usually employed against a very well-rounded offensive attack)
2. Hero (geared for keying and stopping one particular player, such as an outstanding I tailback or option quarterback in the veer)
3. Tandem (fashioned to stop two or three outstanding players who work closely together, such as a quarterback-receiver passing combination)

The Defensive Coordinator must also take into consideration these more specific areas in preparing to defend against an opponent's offense.

1. Defending according to field and boundary tendencies
2. Defending according to formation tendencies
3. Defending according to down and distance tendencies
4. Defending according to pass-run tendencies
5. Defending according to long- and short-yardage tendencies
6. Defending according to goal-line tendencies
7. Defending according to two-minute tendencies
8. Defending according to personnel
9. Defending according to critical situations

Finally, the Defensive Coordinator must choose the basic alignments and adjustments to be used against the opponents, and match these to the aforementioned tendencies and situations in order to formulate a well thought out, aggressive defensive game plan—a game plan that will take away the best that the opponents have first, therefore answering the question, "What Must We Stop?"

## WRAP-UP

The ultimate goal of every Defensive Coordinator is to force the opponents to do just the opposite of their game plan (run when they want to pass, etc.). As this chapter has demonstrated, a well-organized, thoughtfully gathered scout report that is carefully compiled to reveal all the opponent's major tendencies, combined with a strong, well thought out game plan will provide the Defensive Coordinator with the best possible opportunity to stop his opponents. Each segment of the game-plan preparation process should be carried out so that only the important items are evaluated and acted upon. Also, the Defensive Coordinator should, as was mentioned, spend some time instructing the Scouts in what he needs (scout reporting and compilation) to construct a successful defensive game plan.

The Defensive Coordinator should also use all the inexpensive supplementary aids available such as a tape recorder, a one-step camera, and brightly colored posters, etc., to enhance the game plan in every way possible. In conclusion, he should also keep in mind the following items when preparing each game plan:

1. Make the defensive plan flexible.
2. Compensate for each defensive weakness (personnel and those inherent in the basic alignment).
3. Make opponents do what they least like to do.
4. Take advantage of all tip-offs.
5. Remember that most big mistakes can be forced in the opponent's passing game.
6. Plan thoroughly and coach positively, so that the defensive unit can play aggressively and with great spirit and morale.

# 4

# HOW TO ORGANIZE
# THE OFF-SEASON SCOUTING
# PROGRAM
## (Head Coach)

MANY football programs provide off-season training for the next year's players. In such programs, much effort is usually put into the physical and mental development of the players. Many other programs have no specific off-season training period because the coaches work with other sports out of football season. Very often, in either case, coaching staffs fail to devote enough time to a most important phase of the game: off-season pre-scouting of the upcoming season's opponents. Regardless of staff size or out-of-season coaching assignments, there is plenty of time at some point in the school year to develop an excellent off-season scouting program.

## ORGANIZING FOR NEXT SEASON'S OPPONENTS

The key to a successful off-season scouting program is organization. If properly organized, such a program will provide up to a week of intense study per opponent (often more). There must also be time allotted for more general pre-scouting study sessions and for training members of the Scouting Crews. This time, of course, will be time in addition to off-season training periods or the coaching of other sports. A staff's schedule can be arranged so as to allow each coach time (out of his season if he coaches another sport) to work on off-season scouting without taking away a great deal of his spare time. Remember, organization is the key. The following sections illustrate some guidelines for setting up the off-season scouting program.

## Arrange a Tentative Scouting Schedule

After the next season's schedule of opponents is completed and confirmed, the Head Coach should arrange a tentative scouting schedule. (Figures 4-1, 4-2, and 4-3 on pages 49 through 51, show examples of tentative scouting schedules.) In planning such an itinerary, you should keep in mind the following things:

1. If full Scouting Crews are available, assign the best Scouts to the projected best opponents as much as possible.
2. If the Scouting Staff is limited, you may want to schedule your best Scout to see each opponent the week before you play them. (This will complement the material the other Scouts collect.)
3. Schedule Scouting Crews according to which coaches work best together.
4. Be sure to have at least one experienced Scout in each Crew, if possible.
5. Keep in mind that one or more of your Scouting Staff may leave your school for a position on another staff. This possibility may necessitate some rearranging of the tentative scouting schedule, according to the scouting ability of the coach you hire as a replacement.

Once the tentative scouting schedule is completed, the Head Coach should acquaint the Scouts with the pre-scouting program. In doing so, you should explain these following points thoroughly:

1. The tentative scouting schedule;
2. The information needed on each opponent;
3. The information-gathering sources;
4. The file system for each opponent. (See Figure 4-7.)
5. The schedule for off-season pre-scouting meetings.

### Assign Opponents to Varsity Staff Members

Along with implementing the tentative scouting program, the Head Coach should assign the next season's opponents to the members of the Varsity Staff for study. According to the number of coaches on the staff, each coach (including the Head Coach) will have at least two opponents he must study extensively. This Varsity Staff study of the opponents, coordinated with the Scout's work in the pre-scouting program, will furnish an excellent portfolio of pertinent information which will be most important and helpful when the season begins.

Some goals for the Varsity Staff to keep in mind when studying opponents in the off-season are:

1. Regardless of each staff member's coaching area, he should be sure to give full attention to all phases of the opponent's game when studying them.
2. Each staff member should attempt to be totally objective in studying upcoming opponents. This will make for more realistic planning against each opponent's best maneuvers and personnel.
3. Having a thorough knowledge of his personnel, each staff member should evaluate each opponent's returning personnel so as to gain every advantage from this standpoint in planning.
4. Each staff member should attempt to gain every insight possible into the opposing staff's offensive and defensive philosophy, and in doing so, record any year-to-year carryover in major tendencies.
5. All the material gathered by each staff member concerning opponents should be carefully recorded and inserted into the individual file kept on each opponent (Figure 4-7).

### Pre-Scouting Opponents—Full Staff

Of course, the full staff football programs have the optimum advantage in pre-scouting opponents during the off-season. Head Coaches in such programs have enough coaches to assign complete Scouting Crews to the team's next season opponents, and should be able to assign each Varsity Staff member two or three opponents for study. Through this type of pre-scouting program, the full staff is able to pinpoint even the most minute aspects of each opponent's capabilities. Figure 4-4 shows an example of Scouting Crew's and Varsity Staff's assignments in pre-scouting the next season's opponents.

The staff must work around their coaching duties in other sports in developing the off-season pre-scouting program. For example, the basketball coaches will have some time in the spring for pre-scouting assignments. Those coaches who have spring sports coaching assignments can complete their pre-scouting duties before their other sports begin.

In the full staff off-season pre-scouting agenda (Figure 4-4), the tentative scouting schedule is listed by Scouting Crews and the opponents they are tentatively assigned to scout. Also, the Varsity Staff opponent assignments are shown. Finally, a checklist is provided to be sure that all pertinent information is gathered and filed. This Agenda Form may be kept on the coaches' office bulletin board for ease of access for the entire staff. The Head Coach should also keep his own copy for quick reference.

By pre-scouting opponents with Scouting Crews on the one hand and the Varsity Staff on the other hand, the Head Coach can be assured that every possible angle has been covered in the off-season scouting program. In this respect, the full staff has a distinct advantage in such a program because of the number of coaches available.

## Pre-Scouting Opponents—Medium Staff

The medium staff, although it has fewer coaches and those they have are involved more in working with other sports, can do an excellent job of off-season pre-scouting. The major differences in comparison with the full staff method is that there will be fewer Scouts per Crew, fewer Crews and fewer Varsity Staff members to study opponents. This fact will simply require each Crew and each Varsity Staff member to study one or two more opponents.

Taking into consideration the above mentioned facts, the Head Coach will need to do a good job of organizing so as to make use of the time each coach has available. Figure 4-5 illustrates a medium staff off-season pre-scouting agenda.

### Pre-Scouting Opponents—Limited Staff

The Head Coach of a limited staff will need to make some adjustments in his off-season pre-scouting. Some of these adjustments will probably include:

1. Assigning more opponents for each coach to study;
2. Limiting the amount of information gathered on each opponent;
3. Using films, last season's file, and/or discussions with other staffs as the primary sources of information if there are not enough coaches available to pre-scout each opponent individually;
4. Careful scheduling of the off-season pre-scouting program around the coaching of other sports by members of the staff;
5. And because in most cases, less time (in coaching man-hours) is available for pre-scouting each opponent, the Head Coach must have the program well organized so that the information-gathering process is quick and simple.

Figure 4-6 illustrates a possible pre-scouting agenda for a limited staff.

## INSTRUCTING SCOUTS IN SCOUTING TECHNIQUE

The art of proper scouting technique is probably one of the most overlooked and least emphasized phases of most football programs. The off-season is an excellent time for the Varsity Staff to instruct the Scouting Staff in methods to be used in scouting future opponents. Also, before a well-organized and effective off-season pre-scouting program can be implemented, the Scouts must be knowledgeable about the desired scouting procedures so they can properly prepare pre-scouting information in the manner desired by the Head Coach and Varsity Staff.

With these thoughts in mind, devote as much time as is available (according to staff size and out-of-season coaching responsibilities) early in the off-season, to working with the Scouts so that they will be prepared to participate productively in the off-season pre-scouting program. For specific suggestions concerning the instruction of the Scouting Staff, please refer to Chapter 8, "How to Train Coaches Who Scout."

## PREPARING A FILE ON EACH OPPONENT

As the off-season pre-scouting program begins to produce specific information about each opponent, it is wise to establish a file system to keep the material separated and ready for easy reference. Individual opponent files should be kept in order of appearance on the next season's schedule. Figure 4-7 shows an opponent's file checklist, which can be used to properly complete each file.

In preparing off-season pre-scouting files on opponents, there will be two major categories in most cases: continuing opponents and new opponents. Many times, the information-gathering process will vary according to whether the opponents are continuing or new.

### Continuing Opponents

Gathering pre-scouting information on continuing opponents is relatively simple. Use the aforementioned methods to complete the opponent's file checklist which can be done, for the most part, from material already on hand.

### New Opponents

New opponents require more background work to establish file information. For example, coaches from other schools should be contacted so that films, scout reports, etc., can be secured, broken down, and added to each new opponent's file. This process also provides an excellent opportunity to discuss the opponents with these coaches. Much useful information can be gathered in this manner.

## WRAP-UP

Of course, each football program has its own unique situation during the off-season. Some staffs will be almost totally free to work on off-season pre-scouting from the end of the football season until school ends. On the other hand, many other staffs will be almost totally involved with other sports, practically throughout the entire school year. Regardless of the situation, some off-season pre-scouting can and should be done. This chapter is meant only as a guide and these suggestions should be used whenever feasible in each staff's off-season preparation.

There are two suggestions I would like to make concerning the off-season. The first is directed toward the staff which has its team doing off-season drills. The off-season training program can be a "long year" for both coaches and players. To keep players' off-season interest high, mentally preparing for one opponent each week can keep the program lively. Merely devoting the cal or stretching period to "get a Wildcat" for a week, then progressing through the next season's schedule will help. This process can also be carried to any point the staff wishes, such as working on one technique each week that will be used versus a specific opponent the next year.

The second suggestion has to do with staff meetings. According to staff size, available time, and off-season coaching duties, short staff meetings should be held to discuss each opponent after completing the opponent's files through pre-scouting. These meetings can spend from one day to one week per opponent, according to staff size and work load. Ideas from these meetings should be recorded and used when pre-season scouting begins in the fall.

## FULL STAFF SCOUTING SCHEDULE CHART

Year_____

*Team Scouted

(Open Date Not Accounted For – All Coaches Scout)

| | Scouting Crew #1 | Scouting Crew #2 | Scouting Crew #3 | Scouting Crew #4 |
|---|---|---|---|---|
| Sept. 1 | * _____ at _____ Time_____ (Scrimmage) Scouts_____ | _____ at * _____ Time_____ (Scrimmage) Scouts_____ | _____ at * _____ Time_____ (Scrimmage) Scouts_____ | |
| Sept. 8 | At Our Game | * _____ at _____ Time_____ Scouts_____ | * _____ at _____ Time_____ Scouts_____ | _____ at * _____ Time_____ Scouts_____ |
| Sept. 15 | * _____ at _____ Time_____ Scouts_____ | At Our Game | _____ at* _____ Time_____ Scouts_____ | * _____ at _____ Time_____ Scouts_____ |
| Sept. 22 | _____ at * _____ Time_____ Scouts_____ | _____ at* _____ Time_____ Scouts_____ | At Our Game | _____ at* _____ Time_____ Scouts_____ |
| Sept. 29 | * _____ at _____ Time_____ Scouts_____ | * _____ at _____ Time_____ Scouts_____ | * _____ at _____ Time_____ Scouts_____ | At Our Game |
| Oct. 6 | At Our Game | _____ at* _____ Time_____ Scouts_____ | _____ at* _____ Time_____ Scouts_____ | * _____ at _____ Time_____ Scouts_____ |
| Oct. 13 | * _____ at _____ Time_____ Scouts_____ | At Our Game | * _____ at _____ Time_____ Scouts_____ | _____ at* _____ Time_____ Scouts_____ |
| Oct. 20 | _____ at* _____ Time_____ Scouts_____ | * _____ at _____ Time_____ Scouts_____ | At Our Game | * _____ at _____ Time_____ Scouts_____ |
| Oct. 27 | * _____ at _____ Time_____ Scouts_____ | _____ at * _____ Time_____ Scouts_____ | | At Our Game |
| Nov. 3 | At Our Game | * _____ at _____ Time_____ Scouts_____ | | |

Figure 4-1

### MEDIUM STAFF SCOUTING SCHEDULE CHART

Year_____

*Team Scouted

(Open Date Not Accounted For – All Coaches Scout)

Scouting Crew #1                                    Scouting Crew #2

Sept. 1  *_____at_____          _____at*_____
         Time_____(Scrimmage)              Time_____(Scrimmage)

Sept. 8  _____at *_____             *_____at_____
         Time_____                         Time_____

Sept. 15 *_____at_____          _____at*_____
         Time_____                         Time_____

Sept. 22 _____at *_____             *_____at_____
         Time_____                         Time_____

Sept. 29 *_____at_____          _____at*_____
         Time_____                         Time_____

Oct. 6   _____at *_____             *_____at_____
         Time_____                         Time_____

Oct. 13  *_____at_____          _____at*_____
         Time_____                         Time_____

Oct. 20  _____at *_____             *_____at_____
         Time_____                         Time_____

Oct. 27  *_____at_____          _____at*_____
         Time_____                         Time_____

Nov. 3                                           *_____at_____
                                                 Time_____

Figure 4-2

LIMITED STAFF SCOUTING SCHEDULE CHART

Year_____

*Team Scouted

(Open Date Not Accounted For - All Coaches Scout)

One Scouting Crew Or Single Scout Schedule

Sept. 1  *_____ at_____
         Time_____(Scrimmage)

Sept. 8  _____ at *_____
         Time_____

Sept. 15 *_____ at_____
         Time_____

Sept. 22 _____ at *_____
         Time_____

Sept. 29 *_____ at_____
         Time_____

Oct. 6   _____ at *_____
         Time_____

Oct. 13  *_____ at_____
         Time_____

Oct. 20  _____ at *_____
         Time_____

Oct. 27  *_____ at_____
         Time_____

Nov. 3   _____ at *_____
         Time_____

Figure 4-3

FULL STAFF OFF-SEASON PRE-SCOUTING AGENDA

Scouting Crews

Crew #1
Opponents #1, 5, 9

Crew #2
Opponents #2, 6, 10

Crew #3
Opponents #3 & 7

Crew #4
Opponents #4 & 8

Varsity Staff

Head Coach
Opponents #1 & 7

Asst. Coach #1
Opponents #2 & 8

Asst. Coach #2
Opponents #4 & 5

Asst. Coach #3
Opponents #3 & 10

Asst. Coach #4
Opponents #6 & 9

Complete Follow Up on each team. (Check each item completed.)

| Opponent | Last Season's Film Charts | Returning Personnel Chart | Last Season's Game Tendency Chart | Completed File |
|----------|---------------------------|---------------------------|-----------------------------------|----------------|
| 1 | | | | |
| 2 | | | | |
| 3 | | | | |
| 4 | | | | |
| 5 | | | | |
| 6 | | | | |
| 7 | | | | |
| 8 | | | | |
| 9 | | | | |
| 10 | | | | |

Figure 4-4

### MEDIUM STAFF OFF-SEASON PRE-SCOUTING AGENDA

| Scouting Crews | Varsity Staff |
|---|---|
| **Crew #1** | **Head Coach** |
| Opponents 1,3,5,7,9 | Opponents 1,3,7,10 |
| | |
| **Crew #2** | **Asst. Coach #1** |
| Opponents 2,4,6,8,10 | Opponents 2,5,8 |
| | |
| | **Asst. Coach #2** |
| | Opponents 4,6,9 |

**Complete Follow Up on Each Team (Check each item completed.)**

| Opponent | Last Season's Game Film Chart | Returning Personnel Chart | Last Season's Game Tendency Chart | Completed File |
|---|---|---|---|---|
| 1 | | | | |
| 2 | | | | |
| 3 | | | | |
| 4 | | | | |
| 5 | | | | |
| 6 | | | | |
| 7 | | | | |
| 8 | | | | |
| 9 | | | | |
| 10 | | | | |

Figure 4-5

## LIMITED STAFF OFF-SEASON PRE-SCOUTING AGENDA

<u>Scouts</u> (if available)

According to Scouts available,
assign opponents proportionately.
This segment may be phased
into "Staff" if only one scout
is available.

<u>Staff</u>

<u>Head Coach</u>

Opponents #1, 3, 5, 7, 9

<u>Assistant Coach</u>

Opponents #2, 4, 6, 8, 10

Complete Follow Up On Each Team (Check each item completed.)

| Opponent | Last Season's Game Film Charts | Returning Personnel Chart | Last Season's Game Tendency Chart | Completed File |
|----------|-------------------------------|---------------------------|-----------------------------------|----------------|
| 1 | | | | |
| 2 | | | | |
| 3 | | | | |
| 4 | | | | |
| 5 | | | | |
| 6 | | | | |
| 7 | | | | |
| 8 | | | | |
| 9 | | | | |
| 10 | | | | |

Figure 4-6

## NEXT SEASON'S OPPONENTS' FILE CHECK LIST

Opponent To Be Played_____Game#_____Date_____

Nickname_____Colors_____  &_____

1. Scout Report-Game Plan--------------Last Year_____  Others: 19____,19____,19____
2. Post Game Evaluation--------------- Last Year_____  Others: 19____,19____,19____
3. Game Film --------------------------Last Year_____  Others: 19____,19____,19____
4. Film Charts------------------------Last Year_____  Others: 19____,19____,19____
5. Game Off. & Def. Charts------------Last Year_____  Others: 19____,19____,19____
6. Formation Poster(s)----------------Last Year_____  Others: 19____,19____,19____
7. Workout Play Cards (Off. & Def.)---Last Year_____  Others: 19____,19____,19____
8. Personnel Poster-------------------Last Year_____
9. Game Programs ---------------------Last Year_____
10. Returning Personnel Chart _____
11. Newspaper Articles (Stats,etc.)_____

### BASIC INFORMATION

1. Coaches' Ideas (Other Schools) a._____

_____

b._____

_____

c._____

_____

2. Basic Offensive Philosophy a. Type Offense_____

b. Basic Sets (1)_____(2)_____(3)_____

c. Other_____

3. Basic Defensive Philosophy a. Type Defense_____

b. Basic Sets (1)_____(2)_____(3)_____

c. Variations (1)_____(2)_____(3)_____

d. Other:_____

4. Kicking Game  a. Punt--------------------(1)_____(2)_____(3)_____

b. Punt Return------------(1)_____(2)_____(3)_____

c. Kick off----------------(1)_____(2)_____(3)_____

d. Kick Off Return--------(1)_____(2)_____(3)_____

e. Extra Point------------(1)_____(2)_____(3)_____

f. Field Goal--------------(1)_____(2)_____(3)_____

g. Extra Point Def.--------(1)_____(2)_____(3)_____

Figure 4-7

# 5

# HOW TO ORGANIZE
# PRE-SEASON
# SCOUTING PROGRAM
## (Head Coach)

As PLANNING begins in late summer for the upcoming season, and the staff's attention turns to offense, defense, kicking game, personnel, etc., be sure to spend adequate time on preparing the scouting program. A well-organized pre-season scouting process will prove to be very productive and worthwhile as the busy season unfolds.

### FINALIZE AND CONFIRM THE SCOUTING SCHEDULE

The Head Coach or Scouting Coordinator should begin the pre-season scouting program by formulating a final scouting schedule. The finalized scouting schedule should adhere as closely as possible to the off-season scouting schedule so as to keep the same Scouts working on the opponents they have already pre-scouted together.

Once the scouting schedule is finalized, it should be confirmed with the coaches who comprise the scouting staff. The earlier in the summer this is done, the earlier the Scouts can begin to work together in Crews on the opponents they will scout during the season.

### ARRANGE SCOUTING TRIPS AND ACCOMMODATIONS

Another facet of the pre-season scouting process which should be accomplished early is the arranging of the various scouting trips to be made during the upcoming season. Transportation planning should be done early, particularly if school vehicles are to be used. Also, arrangements (and confirmation of them) should be made with the home team so that the Scouts will be able to use press box facilities if available. Taking care of these two items early will prevent problems in the scouting operation during the season.

Another phase of pre-season planning which will prove helpful is the preparation of credentials for each Scouting Crew. A laminated card identifying each Scout and/or a letter of verification for each Crew member will facilitate admission into stadiums and press boxes.

## REVIEW AND UPDATE OFF-SEASON PRE-SCOUTING FILES

After the above-mentioned pre-season preliminaries have been completed, the staff should review every opponent's file and update each one in every way possible. The Scouts can go through the files, view available films and begin to re-familiarize themselves with the opponents they will scout during the season.

Also, various pre-season football publications and newspaper articles will often provide important new information about opponents. This is particularly true in areas where spring training is not permitted and the opponents have not been seen in action since the previous season. Such articles are good for bulletin board display during the season.

The Varsity Staff can also review and update opponent's files. This process should be carried out very thoroughly so that no stone is left unturned in compiling both old and new information on each opponent.

Medium and limited staffs can and should also carry out the above-mentioned file review process. Staff size may limit the thoroughness with which each opponent can be reviewed, but as much time as possible should be spent updating opponent's files. Remember, most of your opponents probably have the same problems regarding staff size, and unless they spend some time updating your file, you will have a distinct advantage over them when the season begins if you spend the time updating opponent's files.

## DESIGNATE INTANGIBLE INFORMATION DESIRED ON EACH OPPONENT

Every football team has its own peculiarities. Many of these idiosyncrasies will surface while reviewing offensive, defensive and kicking game tendencies during pre-season undating of opponent's files. Other tendencies, often more important, must be "picked up" or simply recognized and remembered when the Varsity Staff reviews each opponent. Several elements may be involved in each opposing team's peculiarities. Some examples may include:

### 1. Coaching Staff's Personality and Philosophy

Often, these factors will dictate certain tendencies, particularly in crucial situations. (With continuing opponents, discuss among the staff these characteristics. With new opponents, get as much of this information as possible from coaches of other schools who have played the opponents.)

### 2. Recurring Offensive Reliances

Have particular opponents you will play ever installed new offensive systems, only to go back to some of their former basic maneuvers during a season? If so, they probably will do it again if a new offense is planned.

### 3. Recurring Defensive Reliances

The same thing holds true for defensive systems as does for offensive systems. A team may have a pattern of changing basic defenses while continuing to rely on stunting, or other methods, or even going back to their original set during the season.

### 4. Recurring Personnel Reliances

Do certain opponents continually use the same body-type players in specific postions year after year? If so, certain advantages may be available according to the type of personnel used out of habit by opponents.

### 5. Adjusting Game to Personnel

Does the staff make offensive, defensive and other changes to match the abilities of returning personnel? (If so, these changes and the reasons for them should be recognized quickly and noted for the Varsity Staff.)

### 6. Team Morale and Other Intangibles

How does the opponent react to a loss, a big win, injuries to key personnel? How does the team react to setbacks like a touchdown being called back, turnovers and big penalties? These and other intangibles will be worth checking on as the opponents are scouted during the season.

The above-mentioned factors and possibly others will bear watching closely. It will be worth it to the Varsity Staff to spend some time in schooling the Scouts on what to look for with respect to intangibles while scouting each opponent.

## FINALIZE SCOUTING PROCEDURES AND MATERIALS

After all scouting plans, opponent reviewing, and staff scouting discussions are completed, the scouting materials should be finalized. A suggested checklist of scouting procedures and materials that should be completed during pre-season planning includes:

1. Completing the scouting schedule and making all arrangements
2. Preparing Scouts' credentials
3. Reviewing and updating opponents files by Varsity Staff and Scouts
4. Having the Varsity Staff designate the pertinent information on each opponent that the Scouts must compile
5. Completing the scouting booklets and forms (adding or changing material to meet present needs). See Chapter 7, How to Organize the Scouting Materials," for further information concerning scouting materials.

6. Purchasing and/or gathering other scouting materials
   a. Pencils and pens
   b. Clipboards and notebooks
   c. Paper, posterboard, etc.
   d. Colored marking pens
   e. 3 × 5 or 5 × 8 cards
   f. Glue
   g. Binoculars
   h. Sound recorders
   i. Still snapshot camera
   j. Hole punch
   k. Scissors
   l. Stopwatches
7. For computerized scouting systems, making any arrangements necessary with those involved and gathering any additional materials needed
8. Meeting with Scouts to finalize information wanted on each opponent and to review use of scouting materials, methods and procedures.
9. Meeting with Scouting Crews to finalize responsibilities within each Crew
10. Wrapping up any loose ends which may need attention with respect to the in-season scouting program

## PREPARE TO SCOUT YOUR OWN TEAM

Where staff size allows, or where funds are available for outside scouting sources, the Head Coach should prepare to have his own team scouted. This is an excellent way to check your own tendencies as well as to gain other valuable information about your team which may not otherwise surface. Having access to your own tendencies and other information will be most helpful in future game planning.

The practice of scouting yourself can even be carried on in smaller systems, in which one or more Scouts may be available due to open dates on the regular opponents Scouting schedule. Whatever the means, scouting your own team's games will pay off in the future. More suggestions on scouting your own team follow in Chapter 6 ("How to Organize the In-Season Scouting Program") in the section called "Scouting Yourself."

## REVIEW METHODS WITH SCOUTS

The methods and procedures of scouting and game planning should be reviewed with the Scouts during the pre-season period. The Head Coach, Scouting Coordinator, Offensive Coordinator, Defensive Coordinator and/or any other member of the Varsity Staff who desires specific information can cover the various methods, materials and procedures which will produce the desired results from the scouting program. Add the background information in the opponent's files already digested by the Scouts to a Varsity Staff review of methods and procedures, and the scouting program will be properly prepared for the beginning of the regular season. See Chapter 8 ("How to Train Coaches Who Scout") for further suggestions concerning the training of Scouts.

## WRAP-UP

Excellent planning during the pre-season will pay off during the busy season. It will free the Varsity Staff to concentrate more upon each opponent. It will make the Scouts' jobs easier, and give them more time to spend working on opponents. It will remove any slip-ups which might take valuable time to correct. It will also prepare the Varsity Staff and Scouts thoroughly for each opponent, which will make the in-season program go much more smoothly. The suggestions made in this chapter for pre-season planning are general for the most part. Each staff has its own unique situation to contend with during pre-season preparation. Some staffs will have time to prepare for the scouting program very thoroughly; others will not. Regardless of the situation, any time spent in planning the in-season scouting program will be time well spent.

# 6

## HOW TO ORGANIZE THE IN-SEASON SCOUTING PROGRAM
### (Head Coach)

### PROPER PREPARATION IS THE KEY

Proper, well-organized preparation in the off-season and pre-season phases of the scouting program will make it possible for the Varsity Staff to concentrate exclusively on each opponent during the season. Thorough preparation in the areas of the scouting program mentioned in Chapters 4 and 5 will also enable the Scouts to concentrate their time on scouting opponents, without spending time in unnecessarily preparing materials and the like during the season.

Since time is of the essence during the season, the Head Coach who prepares his staff properly in the off-season and pre-season can be sure that his in-season scouting program will be devoted completely to gaining all the important information about each opponent. If the scouting program is at its proper stage when the season begins, the only areas left for the Scouts to work on, with respect to Varsity Scouting, will be: (1) scouting; (2) compilation; and (3) help with game planning.

### SCOUTING AND FUNDAMENTALS FIRST

The single most important goal or objective of coaches at all levels on a staff should be the success of the Varsity

Program. The success or failure of the Varsity Team will directly affect all coaches, regardless of their postions on a staff.

With this in mind, the Head Coach should emphasize to all assistants who do scouting, the importance of these two main objectives: scouting for the Varsity, and teaching fundamentals to the younger players on the level at which each coach works now. The importance of a good scouting performance cannot be overemphasized to assistant coaches. In many instances, the important information they gather, or fail to gather, makes a difference in the outcome of a game with the opponents they scout. For this reason, it is imperative that the Scouts realize that all phases of the scouting program are a most important and integral part in the overall program.

Departing from the direct scouting aspect for a moment, let us examine another area which, if handled correctly, may well improve the scouting prowess of the entire Scouting Staff. This area is the emphasizing of teaching basic fundamentals at the lower grade levels, rather than pressing to win every game.

Assistant Coaches who are responsible for the lower grade programs should understand that teaching fundamentals to their players and scouting for the Varsity are both more important to the entire program in the long run, than winning is at their level. Of course, winning is important to those involved, but teaching the proper fundamentals to young players will pay larger dividends in the future than winning will at lower levels. Example: A few years ago, we had a 25-game winning streak at the Varsity level which also produced two district championships. The seniors who played on the first championship team won only one game when they were in the eighth grade, and only one game in the ninth grade. The seniors on the second championship team won a total of four games while in the eighth and ninth grades.

The fundamentals they were taught in the lower grades, along with their improving abilities as they matured, combined with a well-organized Varsity program and excellent scouting made the difference. The moral of the story is that Assistant Coaches who scout and coach at lower levels should be instructed and encouraged in the importance of their dual responsibilities: scouting and fundamentals first. When this has been accomplished, the Varsity Staff will benefit from better scouting reports at the present and better players in the future. Assistant Coaches who scout will also be able to do a better job of scouting and coaching without the pressure to win, and knowing they are very valuable to the success of the Varsity program.

## INTERACTION WITHIN A SCOUTING CREW

Whether the individual Scouting Crews consist of one or two coaches on a limited staff, or four coaches per Crew on a full staff, proper interaction within each Crew is very important to the successful scouting of opponents. It will be well worth the Head Coach's or one of the Varsity Coach's time to sit down with each Scouting Crew and solidify the different coaches' weekly duties or assignments with respect to scouting each game. This practice will organize each Crew and will allow the Scouts to decide which coaches can best accomplish each of the various duties. It will also curb any possible hesitation or confusion on the part of the Crews when it is time to scout.

Some of the items which may be assigned or organized within each of the Crews include:

1. Picking up film and projector (for pre-scouting review);
2. Picking up scouting materials (and credentials for entry into stadium), if necessary;
3. Picking up car or transportation to be used on trip;
4. Arranging where the Crew will eat (See Chapter 13, "How to Scout the Game," for further ideas on pre-game meal);
5. Scouting duties at the game
   a. Calling out defense
   b. Recording defense
   c. Calling out offense
   d. Recording offense
   e. How kicking game recording will be handled
   f. How personnel and position recording will be handled
   g. How supplementary materials (tape recorder, stop watch, etc.) will be used
   h. Who will gather pre-game information (on field and in press box)
   i. How half-time and post-game procedures will be handled

    j.   Return of transportation to lot, etc.
    k.  Next-morning compilation methods and duties
    l.   Transfer of information to Varsity Staff and team
    m. Filing of valuable information in opponent's file

Chapter 13 contains further information concerning "at the game" scouting suggestions.

Working out such duties with each crew before the scouting actually begins each season will make for a much smoother and much more productive scouting program during the season. This is true regardless of the size of the staff or the thoroughness with which it is capable of scouting its opponents.

## SCOUTING YOURSELF

As mentioned in Chapter 5, if coaching personnel is available, it will be very productive to scout your own team as many times as possible during the season. This practice will provide your staff with much important information (the same basic information your future opponents gain through scouting your team), and should be carried out, if only for one game with a limited staff, or every game with a full staff.

There are several ways in which the information accumulated by scouting yourself can be used to great advantage. First, every coaching staff sets some type of tendencies in the offensive, defensive and kicking game phases. No matter how much this practice is guarded against, it happens. And, it often happens in the heat of a close game in crucial situations. Also, these tendencies are usually set subconsciously. To have knowledge of such tendencies, a staff should have one or more assistant coaches scout its own games at every opportunity.

From the tendencies that a scout notes, a staff can decide to make some changes which may be necessary to throw opponents who rely heavily on such tendencies off balance in their game planning. This may not seem so important to some coaches, but if the opponents depend on past tendencies (which have been changed through self-scouting), in crucial situations it could mean the difference between winning or losing several close games during a season. This is particularly true with respect to offensive adjustments, which the team can make to change tendencies picked up through self-scouting.

Second, the presence of a staff's own assistant coaches performing a self-scouting function at Varsity games can be very helpful during the game. For example, a quarterly report can be relayed from the Scouts to the Varsity Staff on the sideline, pointing out possible changes or adjustments. The Scouts can also make helpful suggestions at half-time.

Third, if possible, the Scouting Crew who self-scouts its own team should be the same Crew who had previously scouted the opponents being played that night. This will often allow the Scouts more insight into what the opponents will do in certain situations. This information can be relayed to the Varsity Staff, and will help in decision making during crucial situations in the game.

Each coaching staff will also find other advantages accruing from the process of self-scouting. Regardless of the number of Scouts available for self-scouting, or the thoroughness with which this facet of the scouting program is carried out, it is worth whatever effort is necessary to accomplish it.

## WRAP-UP

Preparation and organization are the cornerstones of carrying out a good in-season scouting program. If the proper groundwork is laid in the off-season and pre-season, and the Scouts understand their responsibilities, scouting duties and goals, the in-season scouting program should operate smoothly and be very instrumental in having a successful football season. Scout yourself whenever possible. This source of information about your own team can be very valuable.

This chapter is a guide in getting your own in-season scouting program started. It does not, of course, include all the aspects of in-season scouting. The following chapters cover the major categories of scouting and game planning in much closer detail. Each category is described and discussed carefully with the hope that the reader will gain some positive ideas which will enhance his scouting and game-planning procedure.

# 7

## HOW TO ORGANIZE
## THE SCOUTING MATERIALS
### (Staff)

ORGANIZING the scouting materials is one of the most important factors in producing a thorough, well-rounded scouting and game-planning program. This chore is often overlooked and pushed into the background until the last minute, but the proper organization and preparation of scouting materials will help set the stage for a successful season when given the right priority.

### OFF-SEASON AND PRE-SEASON PREPARATION

During the off-season, as opponent's files are being compiled, the Head Coach and the Varsity Staff should spend some time making any changes they deem necessary in the basic scouting forms and materials. Reviewing scouting materials while working on opponent's files may stimulate some positive ideas for changing the materials to better reveal important information. After reviewing the scouting materials and making any necessary changes, the materials should be prepared and filed, so they are ready for use in the fall. This is also a good time to update supplementary scouting materials. Also, the Varsity Staff can spend some time with the Scouts, reviewing the use of the newly prepared scouting materials.

In the pre-season, the scouting materials should be prepared by the Scouting Crews for use during the season. At this time also, a check-out list can be prepared to keep up with the materials, particularly the supplementary materials. Another review of the use and purpose of the scouting materials should be carried out with the Scouts, and particularly with any assistant coaches who are new to the staff. This will insure a better job by the Scouts during the season.

Most of the materials which will be discussed in this chapter are also discussed in other chapters which relate specifically to particular facets of scouting and game planning. Therefore, these scouting materials will be discussed here only in an organizational and preparatory context to provide a guide for a more detailed treatment of these materials. Other materials and forms, such as the cover sheet for the scouting booklet (Figure 7-1), will be discussed and illustrated in this chapter only.

## THE SCOUTING BOOKLET

Most scouting systems use some type of booklet as the basic instrument from which their Scouts work. Ideally, such a booklet should be:

1. Functional—properly prepared for use by Scouts. It must produce the desired information.
2. Inclusive but consise—it must include all the material necessary to gather the proper information, and also be brief and to the point, so that time and energy are not wasted on unimportant matters.
3. Easy to compile—categories must be organized and arranged for ease in the compilation of information process.

A well-organized scouting booklet will most likely include at least the following items (some staffs may be more specific):

1. Appropriate cover sheet. (Figure 7-1 shows a simple cover sheet.) The cover sheet should meet the needs of the Varsity Staff and be functional or there is no use for it.
2. Pre-game and general information sheet. (Figure 7-2 illustrates a pre-game information sheet. Further information and diagrams concerning pre-game information can be found in Chapter 9.)

3. Offensive and defensive personnel sheet. (Figure 7-3 depicts an offensive and defensive personnel sheet. Further information concerning personnel can be found in Chapters 9, 10, 11 and 12.)

4. Offensive general information sheet. (Figure 7-4 shows an example of an offensive general information sheet. This information will be discussed further in Chapter 14.)

5. Defensive general information sheet. (Figure 7-5 illustrates a defensive general information sheet. See Chapters 11 and 14 for further information and illustrations concerning the defense.)

6. Kicking game sheets. (Figures 7-6 and 7-7 depict examples of kicking game sheets. Further information and illustrations concerning the kicking can be found in Chapter 12.)

## GAME RECORDING MATERIALS

An excellent stock of at-the-game recording materials for the Scouting Staff can be accumulated at minimal cost. Of course, a great deal of the recording material will be devised by the Varsity Staff to meet the specific needs of its own scouting/game-planning program. A suggested list of recording items, other than the scouting booklet, may include

1. Play-by-play recording cards or sheets (offense, defense and kicking game);
2. Clipboards and/or notebooks;
3. Plenty of pencils and pens;
4. Special sheets for tip-offs, unusual action, etc.;
5. Any other specific information sheets (such as defensive variations and stunts);
6. Sound tape recorder (if this method is incorporated with written scouting system);
7. Extra paper for important notes, etc.

More specific suggestions concerning recording materials can be found in Chapters 10, 11, 12 and 13.

## COMPILATION AND GAME-PLANNING MATERIALS

The materials used in compiling scouting information and planning for upcoming opponents can be very varied in scope. The wide range of activities involved in the phases of compilation and game planning necessitate several categories of material. Following is a list of materials that may be used in the processes of compilation and game planning.

1. Film of opponents (and all accumulated scouting information)
2. Play-by-play confirmation sheets (for offense, defense and kicking game—to be used in conjunction with films to confirm and enhance scouting information)
3. Accumulative summarizing sheets and materials (for combining scouting information accumulated from two or more games)
4. Tendency sheets (for running tendencies on opponent's offense, defense, kicking game, personnel and tip-offs);
5. Final compilation forms (for total summary of all information into transferable form for Varsity Staff)
6. Poster board (for various charts, offensive and defensive alignments, best plays, personnel displays, goal setting and film grading systems)
7. Colored pens (for color charts, personnel displays, colorful displays of opponents' alignments, plays, etc., color coding materials by games scouted and, for preparing workout play cards)
8. Game-planning forms (for finalizing and recording all aspects of game plans for upcoming opponents)
9. Workout schedules, play cards, etc. (all the planning materials used in preparing on-the-field workouts in preparation for upcoming opponents)

## SUPPLEMENTARY SCOUTING MATERIALS

The area of supplementary scouting materials is one in which a staff can make great strides in making its scouting/game-planning program as productive as possible. The following are suggestions for supplementary scouting materials.

1. Sound tape recorders (can be used for a variety of purposes in scouting/game planning such as recording play-by-play, notations of personnel, tip-offs, etc., as an aid to compilation and as an aid to the Head Coach and Varsity Staff in a variety of operations in game planning)

2. Binoculars (for close-up viewing of personnel, techniques, alignments, etc.)
3. Stopwatches (for timing the kicking game—center snap, getting kick away, hang time, personnel covering kicks. Also for checking huddle time of opponents and other related maneuvers)
4. One-step camera (for snapping still photos of opponents' alignments and formations from the screen as film is being viewed)
5. Computer (regardless of the type of computer system used, whether simple or complex, this method of scouting can ease the burden of compilation and provide many cross-referenced tendencies)
6. Hole punches and triangle clippers (for use as a a tendencying tool when segmented scouting play-by-play cards are used)

### WRAP-UP

The category of scouting materials is so broad a spectrum that there is no way to list or discuss all the items involved. This chapter is meant simply to serve as a guide for the staff in securing, organizing and preparing the scouting materials.

Also, the chapter is written with the needs of a medium to full staff in mind, using the standard system of scouting. Computerized systems and some full staffs will likely use more materials which may feature greater detail, while most limited staffs may use fewer materials with less detail.

The important thing to remember about scouting materials is that proper preparation in the off-season and preseason will eliminate any delay or confusion during the busy regular season when efficiency in the scouting process is so necessary for success.

SCOUTING BOOKLET COVER SHEET

TEAM SCOUTED_____vs._____

DATE_____TIME_____PLACE_____

FIELD CONDITION_____WEATHER_____WIND_____

SCOUTS_____

COLOR OF UNIFORMS: PANTS_____JERSEY_____

NUMBER IN UNIFORM_____ORGANIZATION_____SPIRIT_____

CAPTAINS_____

OTHER COMMENTS:

Figure 7-1

PRE-GAME INFORMATION SHEET

Opponent Scouted:_____

Colors: _____ & _____
                pants                    jerseys

Wind and weather: _____

Condition of field: _____

Captains: _____

Passers:  Name_____Number_____

          _____    _____

          _____    _____

          Circle:    Long      Short      Fast    Accurate    Inac.
          Circle:    Right handed         Left Handed

Punters:  Name_____Number_____

          _____    _____

          _____    _____

          Average distance_____Fast   Slow   Long   Short
          High   Low    Right    Left
          Right Foot    Left Foot
          Center snap: good    fair    poor    slow    fast
          Do they Quick Kick? yes   no

Extra Point: poor    fair    fast    slow
          Name_____Number_____

          _____    _____

          _____    _____

Kickoff: Teed up  yes  no   Avg. distance_____right   left   mid.
          Name_____Number_____

          _____    _____

          _____    _____

Pass Receivers: Name_____Number_____good   fair   poor
                _____    _____good   fair   poor
                _____    _____good   fair   poor
                _____    _____good   fair   poor
                _____    _____good   fair   poor
                _____    _____good   fair   poor

Comments: General appearance                Spirit

Gossip:

Figure 7-2

OFFENSIVE AND DEFENSIVE PERSONNEL SHEET

Opponent Scouted_____vs_____Date_____

Offensive Line Up                                Diagram Offensive Huddle

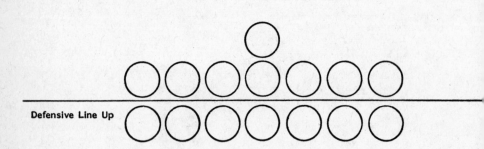

Defensive Line Up

Figure 7-3

OFFENSIVE GENERAL INFORMATION SHEET

Opponent Scouted_____

1.  Do they check off plays?                    If so, to what?


2.  What is their cadence or snap count?      Different kinds?

    a. Do they go on first sound?

    b. How often?

    c. On passing downs?

3.  What kind of splits does the offensive line take?    (Distance, show on diagram)


4.  Do they go from an up position?          Explain.


5.  Do they flex the ends?                    Distance and situation and how often?


6.  Any keys from QB mechanics?              Hands under?


7.  Do they shift formation?                  From what to what?


8.  Do they use motion?                       Diagram.



9.  Distance receivers split on each formation?  Diagram.



10. Estimate speed of split receivers individually.

11. Draw all pass routes, giving exact depth of cuts.

12. Do receivers go from up position at all?

Figure 7-4

## DEFENSIVE GENERAL INFORMATION SHEET

1. Strong corner

   a. How far off wide receiver? _____
   b. Does he come up and bump the receiver? _____
   c. Does he ever roll up from the outside and force quickly? _____
   d. Is the roll coverage disguised? _____
   e. What kind of speed does he have? _____

2. Strong safety

   a. Does he take the pitch or roll to deep 1/3 most? _____
   b. Can we crackback on him? (How deep does he line up)? _____
   c. Do they play man for man? _____
   d. Do they use cover 5? (5 underneath and 2 deep) _____

3. Weakside corner

   a. How far off wide receiver? _____
   b. On flow toward him, does he take deep 1/3 or does he come up to force? _____

   c. If force, up to what width? _____

4. Free safety

   a. What is his basic alignment? _____
   b. Can he cover veer pass? _____
   c. Does he ever take pitch man to weak side? _____
   d. Speed? _____

## DEFENSIVE FRONT OBSERVATIONS

## GENERAL OBSERVATIONS

Figure 7-5

PUNTING GAME SHEET

PUNTING

1. Type of punt formation:  spread     tight     end split     quick kick.

2. How far do they kick?_____

3. Who is down first?_____

4. Do they run or pass from this formation ?  yes    no

5. Do they cover fast,    med,    slow?

6. Which way can we run it back?  right     left.

Punt Receiving

1. Can we quick kick on them?   yes    no

2. Do they tip-off the return?  yes   no

3. Do they hand off?   yes    no

4. Who is their most dangerous receiver?_____

5. Do they fair catch?   yes    no

6. Can we run or pass against their punt defense?  yes   no

Diagram punt formations

Diagram receiving formation

Figure 7-6

KICKOFF GAME SHEET

**Kickoff Coverage:**

1. Draw alignment. (Get numbers, if possible)
2. Who is the safety?_____
3. Any crossing of men as they go downfield?  yes   no (If yes, diagram it)
4. Average depth of kick?_____

---

**Kickoff Return:**

1. Draw alignment with numbers of deep receivers.
2. Return mostly to:  Middle,   Right,    Left.
3. Wedge up the middle or cross blocking?
4. Any reverses or trick returns?

Figure 7-7

# 8

## HOW TO TRAIN COACHES WHO SCOUT
### (Staff and Scouts)

ONE of the most important and yet often overlooked areas in all of football coaching is the proper training of assistant coaches who make up the Scouting Staff. No Head Coach would begin the season by sending a completely inexperienced secondary coach out to work with that important group without being sure the coach was well drilled in the techniques and type of play the Head Coach desires. Yet, every season coaches are sent out to perform the all-important duty of scouting with little or no instruction in the actual art of scouting. Time spent in instructing the Scouts in proper technique will more than pay for itself.

### SCOUTING PERSONNEL IS ALL-IMPORTANT

The Head Coach should screen applicants very carefully when hiring assistant coaches. This is particularly true if these coaches will be scouting as part of their coaching duties. The Head Coach is not always in total control of personnel hiring, but he should try to have some input on hiring assistant coaches who will take their jobs of coaching and scouting seriously. Also, as was mentioned in Chapter 6, the Scouts presently on the staff should be aware of the importance of their scouting duties and be willing to carry them out to the best of their abilities.

Following are some of the qualities a Head Coach should look for when assigning an assistant coach to the Scouting Staff:

1. Dedication
2. Willingness to work
3. Sound knowledge of basic football (offense, defense, formations, techniques and the like)
4. Quickness to pick up variations from the usual
5. Ability to scrutinize and evaluate opponents quickly
6. Good recording ability (trusting nothing to memory)
7. Ability to work under pressure, play after play
8. Knowing how to separate important information from the unimportant
9. Capability to assimilate and compile information and be able to transfer it in concise, understandable fashion to the Varsity Staff
10. An adventuresome spirit (seeking to secure every possible morsel of information about an opponent any way possible within legal and ethical bounds)

Many Scouts will not possess all the above-mentioned qualities in the beginning, but if the Head Coach selects his assistant coaches judiciously, they will be willing and anxious to improve their scouting capabilities.

## MAKING SCOUTING COUNT

The worst thing that can happen to a well-organized scouting program is for the Varsity Staff to ignore or make less than the best use of scout reports gathered and compiled by the Scouting Staff. I have seen this occur in several situations and I feel sure many other coaches have also. Nothing can discourage, irritate and alienate Scouts more than this. It will also lead to dissention which will spread throughout a staff quickly.

From the beginning, during the off-season (or pre-season if new coaches have been hired) the Head Coach must emphasize the importance of an excellent scouting program to the Varsity Staff as well as to the Scouting Staff. Then, the Head Coach and Varsity Staff should train the Scouting Staff thoroughly in the techniques necessary to produce the desired results from the scouting program. If these things are done, everyone involved will be working towards the same goals, and the Scouts will feel like they are in part responsible for any successes the Varsity Team has. It is very important that the Scouts do a good job and that their work is used in conjunction with the game plan. This is a most important building block on the way to a productive scouting program.

To perpetuate a meaningful scouting program, the Head Coach and Varsity Staff must outline for the Scouts the following categories:

1. Overall purpose of the scouting program
2. Methods to be used
3. Desired results
4. What these results will produce

The specifics within the above-mentioned major categories will certainly vary from staff to staff, but these four major areas should be discussed comprehensively with the Scouting Staff before actual work begins, if the scouting program is to be totally meaningful and successful.

## TRAIN SCOUTS WITH THE ENTIRE VARSITY STAFF

The Head Coach and every member of the Varsity Staff should have a hand in training the Scouting Staff. This is the only means by which a staff can expect proper results from its scouting program. The Head Coach wants a well-rounded, complete scout report on each opponent; the Defensive Coordinator wants to know everything possible about the opponent's offense; the Offensive Coordinator wants a thorough report on the opponent's defense; and any other coaches on the staff want information which aids them in their specific areas.

Each member of the Varsity Staff, therefore, should spend time instructing the Scouts in specific areas, while the Head Coach covers the overall program and any other areas he deems necessary. This process will get the scouting program off on the right foot and insure better results.

## TEACH SPECIFIC SCOUTING TECHNIQUES

Lay the proper technical groundwork with respect to scouting by having the Varsity Staff teach the Scouts the exact scouting techniques to be used. (Some of the more experienced Scouts may already have systems they use while scouting. Allowances should be made in such cases to permit improvisation as long as the necessary information is gathered and is compilable within the Varsity Staff's system.)

The basic categories which may be covered in scouting technique teaching sessions include

1. The week before the game (pre-scouting review and preparation);
2. Gathering scouting materials;
3. The trip (make it meaningful);
4. Pre-game operation (organization is a must);
5. Recording play-by-play;
6. Half-time and post-game organization;
7. Reviewing and compiling scouting information;
8. Transferring compiled information to Varsity Staff (and players in many cases);
9. Scouts' part in game planning;
10. Scouting yourself (if personnel available).

In instructing Scouts, the Varsity Staff may be very specific in such areas as: (1) the recording of play by play; (2) the compiling of information; and (3) the transferring of compiled information to the Varsity Staff. For example, the Offensive and Defensive Coordinators will want to instruct the Scouts closely in the techniques of recording

1. Down and distance
2. Field and hash positions
3. Formations or alignments
4. Type play or defensive action
5. Result of play (ball carrier, passer, receiver or stunts, secondary rotation, etc.)
6. Personnel, substitutions and injury notes
7. Unusual sets, alignments or occurrences
8. Tip-offs

These and other specific areas should be covered by the Varsity Staff, according to the particular needs of the scouting system being used and the philosophy of the Staff. (Chapters 9 through 15 contain more specific information on scouting and compilation methods which may be helpful in the training of Scouts.)

During the instruction, all the scouting materials should be thoroughly explained and demonstrated so the Scouts will know the exact purpose and use of each instrument involved. This is also a good time for providing and demonstrating a shorthand system (if one is used) which will make the Scouts' jobs easier and make it possible to gather much more information. Any shorthand system which improves speed of note-taking will be very worthwhile. Any other facets of the scouting program such as use of supplementary scouting materials should also be covered at this time.

## TEACH SCOUTS ABOUT YOUR SYSTEM
## AND PERSONNEL

The Varsity Staff must also acquaint and instruct the Scouts in the Varsity's offensive, defensive and kicking game systems, if the best possible scouting results are to be expected. If Scouts are thoroughly knowledgeable of the Varsity's systems, they will be able to better pick out the areas in the opponent's game that can be taken advantage of.

Also, the Scouting Staff should be fully acquainted with the Varsity personnel. Each player's strengths and weaknesses should be known by the Scouts. This knowledge will enable the Scouts to make notes about the opponent's personnel in comparison with their own, which will help the Varsity Staff plan to take advantage of certain personnel mismatches, or to compensate for any personnel mismatches in which the opponents have the advantage.

## OFF-SEASON AND PRE-SEASON PRACTICE

For the Scouting Staff, there are many opportunities to practice the art of scouting, compiling and the correct use of the scouting materials during the off-season and pre-season. Proper encouragement and help by the Head Coach and Varsity Staff will make this facet of the scouting program very fruitful when the regular season begins.

Aside from the experience the Scouts will get in helping prepare files on opponents in the off-season, and reviewing and updating the files in the pre-season, other methods of gaining scouting practice out-of-season include

1. Scouting own Varsity's intra-squad scrimmages during spring training (if held) and early fall practice;
2. Scouting college and/or professional games (if nearby);
3. Scouting post-season playoff games between other high schools;
4. Scouting television games (not a lifelike scouting experience, but instant replay provides the Scout with an opportunity to check his work—this is better than nothing, especially in late summer pre-season);
5. Scouting from film (all aspects are not always visible, but rerunning the film helps Scout check his work—again, this is better than nothing and is good during off-season).

It will be good if experienced Scouts can work with the inexperienced ones in these phases of training, and if members of the Varsity Staff can also work with new scouts when the Varsity is not playing or practicing.

## WRAP-UP

No Scout can be expected to do a productive job of scouting unless he knows precisely what is wanted by the Varsity Staff and how he is to accumulate, assimilate and compile this information. Although the Head Coach and Varsity Staff have a very busy year-round job in preparing and coaching their team, a little extra time spent on instructing Scouts in the proper ways to gather desired information will pay big dividends every game day.

The instruction of Scouts will also help the Varsity Coaches become better organized in their own particular phases of the game. (As you have probably realized, any time you have to outline a subject and instruct others in that subject, your own mind becomes keener in the organization and knowledge of the subject.)

Remember, every minute spent instructing the Scouting Staff will eventually be worth at least ten minutes of valuable time during the busy regular season.

# 9

# HOW TO GATHER PRE-GAME AND GENERAL INFORMATION
## (Staff and Scouts)

### THE PRELIMINARIES

"ARRIVE properly prepared" should be a Scouting Crew's motto when scouting a football game. In this case, proper preparation will very generally include

1. Pre-trip review of opponent's file;
2. Gathering and organizing scouting materials;
3. If possible, taking pre-game meal at a restaurant where the opponent's fans may be eating. (Pick up gossip about opponents—this is often very helpful);
4. Arriving at the field at least one hour before game time—purchase at least five game programs;
5. Making film exchange or any other necessary acknowledgments with opponent's staff;
6. Having part of the Scouting Crew remain on the endline or sideline to gather warm-up information—part of Crew should reserve space in press box and begin recording pre-game information;
7. Discussing opponents who are being scouted with other scouts, coaches or reporters who may have seen the team play. (Even the minutest scrap of information may prove important later.)

See Chapter 13 for more specific suggestions concerning pre-game scouting preparation.

## GENERAL INFORMATION

Figures 9-1 and 9-2 show examples of pre-game and general information-gathering forms. The "general information" category often contains some very specific information. For example, the Scouts on or near the field during the warm-up period can pick up much important information, including

1. Size of opponents (Is the game program basically correct concerning players' weights, or are they larger or smaller than listed?)
2. Team spirit and enthusiasm
3. Leaders (Who are the team captains or other leaders? Who is at the heart of the opponent's spiritual and mental hub? This is very important to note. Then, during game, note the specific situations in which this player or group of players is in the line up. What about their offensive, defensive, kicking games?)
4. Injuries (Who, what type and to what extent?)
5. Snap count or cadence (This is very important. Record the basic count, variations, percent of first sound, second sound, etc. Do they appear too audible or automatic? Also, pick up any terms used in commanding defensive maneuvers.)
6. Player mannerisms (Try to note anything unusual done by quarterbacks or other players which may help tip the type of play being run.)
7. Basic widths, depths of alignments (depth of running backs, line splits and any other exact alignment information)
8. Personal characteristics (Which players seem to be mentally toughest, make best contact, take command? Which players seem to have mental lapses, bad hands, shrink from contact, let small injuries bother them?)

While the Scouts on or near the field are gathering this and any other information from the opponent's warm-up period, the Scouts in the press box should be recording such general information as

1. Weather conditions (important—a wet ball, muddy field or high winds often may alter your opponent's game plan entirely)
2. Opponent's colors (jerseys, pants, helmets)
3. Size of squad (number of players suited up)
4. Discuss the opponents thoroughly with other scouts who have seen them play and record this information. (Do this early if possible or as time allows.)

If doing the scouting alone, the Scout will have to be more discerning about which of the above bits of information he should record, because it is not likely that he will be able to get it all. For example, it is much more important to record all phases of the opponent's snap count than it is to record the color of their jerseys and pants. Get the most important information first.

As soon as the most desirable general information is recorded, the Scouts should record information concerning the various phases of the opponent's warm-up specialty sessions.

## KICKING GAME WARM-UP

### Punting

In recording the opponent's punting game warm-up, the following information should be secured:

1. Numbers of all punting game personnel (snappers, punters, punt receivers)
2. Timing of snap (with stopwatch, time each snap by each snapper)
3. Timing of punt (with stopwatch, time each punter from snap to foot contact with football)
4. Timing of hang time (with stopwatch, time each punt for hang time in air)
5. Punter's depth from L.O.S.
6. Numbers of steps punter takes
7. Punter's hands (Does he often drop or mishandle snaps?)
8. Snapper's mannerisms (Any tip-off as to when snap is coming?)

9. Punt receivers (Any information on receivers, judgment, hands, moves, speed.)

## Kickoff

1. Numbers of all kickoff personnel (kickers, receivers)
2. Type tee (Is ball teed up? Do they use an elevated tee or a short tee? Do they ever kick from hold?)
3. Soccer style or conventional?
4. Practice onsides kick? (Where kicked, what type)
5. Average depth of kickoffs (also longest and shortest kicks)
6. Where on field (What part of field do most kicks go to—left, middle, right?)
7. Kick from middle or hash
8. Height and hang time of kick
9. Kickoff receivers

## Extra Point and Field Goal

1. Numbers of all personnel (snappers, holders, kickers)
2. Depth of holder from L.O.S.
3. Kicker's number of steps
4. Timing of snap (with stopwatch, time snaps, to holder's hands)
5. Timing of kick (with stopwatch, time kick from snap to ball clearing L.O.S.)
6. Soccer style or conventional?
7. Does kick gain great height immediately?
8. Accuracy (Extra point. On field goal, record accuracy from depths and hash marks kicked from.)

## PASSING GAME WARM-UP

## Passers

1. Numbers of all passers
2. Dropback or sprint out (If both, best at which one?)
3. Number of steps to set up
4. Right or left hand passer?
5. Release (quick or slow; overhand or sidearm?)
6. Best passes (short or long; curl, out, post, etc.)
7. Accuracy

8. Does anyone pass other than quarterbacks (sweep or option pass possibility)?
9. Mannerisms (licking fingers, etc.—possible tip-offs)

## Receivers

1. Numbers of all receivers
2. Hands (excellent, good, poor, etc.)
3. Speed
4. Best routes
5. Mannerisms (possible tip-off to pass plays)

## LINE WARM-UP

Careful watching of the opponent's linemen in pre-game drills may provide certain valuable information which can be followed up for verification during the game. Examples of information which may be picked up in pre-game line drills include

1. Overall size of offensive or defensive units;
2. Individual and unit quickness;
3. Pulling ability and techniques;
4. Blocking or defensive reaction techniques;
5. Mobility;
6. Personnel mannerisms which may tip off type of play being run;
7. Any other information which may prove helpful.

## TEAM WARM-UP

When the opponents come together for team offensive and/or defensive timing drills, the Scouts can accumulate a wealth of pre-game information which will be very important and helpful once the game begins. Included in the information which can be secured in team pre-game drills are

1. Basic formations or defensive alignments;
2. Starting personnel (and replacements if opponents run two offensive and/or defensive units);
3. Basic plays or defensive adjustments, secondary alignments;

4. Line splits;
5. Unit quickness off the ball;
6. Timing capabilities;
7. Personnel mannerisms which may be keys or tip-offs to type of play being run;
8. Huddle time and how to pick up key man for strongside alignment;
9. Any other information which may be revealing.

## HOW TO PICK UP TIP-OFFS

Often overlooked in the rapid-fire process of scouting, are tip-offs of upcoming offensive, defensive or kicking game maneuvers which, if detected, could be very important to the Varsity Staff when planning for the opponents. These tip-offs may be as individual and small as a receiver licking his fingers before pass plays, or as team-oriented as the running of only one or two specific plays every time the opponents align in a particular offensive formation. Some tip-offs, such as the last example mentioned, may overlap with the tendency category, but the important thing is that the information is recorded somewhere in the scout report and passed on to the Varsity Staff.

## A SPIRIT OF ADVENTURE IS ESSENTIAL

To be good at picking up tip-offs, in fact, just to be a good scout in general, a coach should have some sense of adventure in doing his job. If a Scout is excited about bringing back a complete, well-worked scout report, and has an adventuresome spirit, he is likely to do a good job and pick up several worthwhile tip-offs about the opponents while doing so. In fact, I would rather have a less experienced coach who is fired-up about scouting a game, than a more experienced coach who just goes through the motions of scouting.

The coach who is just doing his job may correctly record all the surface data, but the coach who is adventuresome and excited about his job will often uncover information in the form of tip-offs, which will be valuable in planning for the opponents. It should be a real source of pride for a Scout to pick up certain tip-offs which help his team defeat the opponents he has scouted. To sum up the search for tip-offs, the Scout should be continually alert for anything, no matter how small it may seem, which may give his team an advantage when playing the opponents.

## WRAP-UP

The pre-game and general information portion of scouting is very important. This warm-up period will reveal the personality of a team as well as the specific capabilities of all the specialty groups and finally, give a preview of the team's offense and/or defense before even one play is actually run.

Of course, each Varsity Staff will want a little different information from this area of scouting. Regardless of the type material required, the pre-game information, if secured properly, is in itself a mini-scout report which will be very valuable in the overall scope of the entire scout report. For this reason, expend whatever effort is necessary to gain all the pre-game information possible in a most thorough manner.

PRE-GAME INFORMATION SHEET

Opponent Scouted_____ vs. _____ Date _____

### Punters

| Name | No. | No. of Steps | Dist. from line kick made | Speed in getting kick off | Dist. of kick | Ability |
|------|-----|--------------|---------------------------|---------------------------|---------------|---------|
|      |     |              |                           |                           |               |         |
|      |     |              |                           |                           |               |         |
|      |     |              |                           |                           |               |         |

### Passers

| Name | No. | Type of Pass | Characteristics & Ability |
|------|-----|--------------|---------------------------|
|      |     |              |                           |
|      |     |              |                           |
|      |     |              |                           |

### Receivers

| Name | No | Pos. | Speed & Ability | Remarks |
|------|-----|------|-----------------|---------|
|      |     |      |                 |         |
|      |     |      |                 |         |
|      |     |      |                 |         |
|      |     |      |                 |         |
|      |     |      |                 |         |

### Place Kick

| Name | No. | Dist. Back | Speed | Ability |
|------|-----|------------|-------|---------|
|      |     |            |       |         |
|      |     |            |       |         |

### Kick Off

| Name | No. | Height | Distance | Consistency |
|------|-----|--------|----------|-------------|
|      |     |        |          |             |
|      |     |        |          |             |
|      |     |        |          |             |

Figure 9-1

## PRE-GAME INFORMATION SHEET

Opponent Scouted_____vs_____

Scouts_____

_____

_____

## WARM-UP

| Punters | No. | Distance | Height | Speed | Foot |
|---|---|---|---|---|---|
| 1. | | | | | |
| 2. | | | | | |

| Place Kickers | No. | Distance | Accuracy | Speed | Foot |
|---|---|---|---|---|---|
| 1. | | | | | |
| 2. | | | | | |

| Kick-Off | No. | Distance | Height | | Foot |
|---|---|---|---|---|---|
| 1. | | | | | |
| 2. | | | | | |

| Passers | No. | Evaluation | Throw Deep | | Hand |
|---|---|---|---|---|---|
| 1. | | | | | |
| 2. | | | | | |

| Best Receivers | No. | Speed | Good Hands |
|---|---|---|---|
| 1. | | | |
| 2. | | | |
| 3. | | | |
| 4. | | | |
| 5. | | | |

General Information

Figure 9-2

# 10

# HOW TO SCOUT THE OFFENSE
## (Staff and Scouts)

UNDOUBTEDLY, the most exciting and rapidly paced facet of the football scouting procedure is the recording of the upcoming opponent's offensive game, play by play. A great deal of information is needed on each play in order to correctly determine the opponent's offensive tendencies. To make the play-by-play game progression meaningful, the Scouting Crew must first gather all available information concerning the opponent's offensive personnel and add to this information throughout the game.

## OFFENSIVE PERSONNEL

Actually, most of the offensive personnel information can be gathered in the pre-game team offensive warm-up. When the opponents are running through their basic offensive maneuvers, they probably will run with at least two teams. This gives the Scouting Crew an opportunity to list the opponents two-deep. (The personnel phase of information gathering is covered in depth in Chapter 9.) Figure 10-1 indicates an additional personnel chart which may be helpful in keeping up with personnel changes throughout the game that is being scouted.

### Offensive Starters

Within the Scouting Crew, the Scouting Coach who is designated to list the offensive personnel should be sure to write down the number of each offensive starter. If this is done during the pre-game warm-up, the information should be checked for validity upon the opponent's first offensive possession.

If the opponents are being scouted for the second or third time, the Scout should check and note any personnel changes from previous games. He should also try to find the reason for the changes (injury, loss of position, disciplinary action, change in offensive attack plan, etc.).

## Replacements

Replacements or substitutions play a very large part in many teams' offensive schemes. If this is true in your opponent's case, it is the Scout's job to find out how and why. For example, if a very speedy flanker replacement only plays on downs when the opponents are likely to throw, or run a flanker reverse, etc., it should be noted. This information should be recorded in terms that will be remembered easily, for it could mean the difference between a win or a loss when the Scout's team plays the opponents who are being scouted.

Using the Offensive Personnel Worksheet (Figure 10-1), be sure to note the following things about offensive replacements:

1. Name and jersey number;
2. Position played (sometimes replacements play two or more positions);
3. Reason for change (if known);
4. Special alignment or play action carried out by the replacement or the team as a result of the replacement's presence;
5. Replacement's abilities as opposed to the starter he replaced.

## Key Man

Most offensive teams will have one player or a tandem of players who go to the strong side of the offensive formation in each offensive set. Getting the following information concerning the opponent's key man is very important.

1. Name and jersey number of strongside key man
2. Positions by formations
3. Motion or shift (changing strength of formation)

4. Replacements' names and jersey numbers (very important if aligning defensively according to the key man or his replacements)
5. If double wing, double slot or multiple motion sets are employed by the opponents, note anything that may show a strength of formation for alignment purposes.

With this valuable information, the Defensive Coordinator will be able to set his defensive alignments more carefully in the game plan. (Figure 10-2 shows some basic offensive formations with the key man, denoted by a "K".)

## RECORDING PLAY BY PLAY

In discussing the play-by-play recording of an opponent's offense, we will break the process down into three categories: (1) computer systems (for staffs who use any type computer scouting system, sophisticated or simple); (2) full to medium size staffs which use any type of standard scouting system and; (3) limited size staffs which scout with only one man and use a standard scouting system.

### Computer Scouting Systems

There are probably as many types of computer scouting systems as there are computer systems. The secret to computer scouting is not necessarily the type of system used, but what the staff gains from the computerized report. Remember, a computer can only assimilate the information which is fed into it.

With this in mind, the staff that uses or is considering using a computerized scouting system should carefully consider these things:

1. What information is actually wanted?
2. What information is actually needed?
3. What information is actually helpful?
4. What information will be bulky and useless?
5. What size is the staff and how much can you do with the information once you have it?

Computer scouting is very helpful if you know exactly what you want, what you can use, and how you plan to use it. So much information can be compiled and organized by computer scouting methods (computers can turn out 600 lines of information a minute today), that it should be regulated by each staff according to need, usefulness and staff size.

Figure 10-3 illustrates a basic scouting form which is used to gather and compile information for programming a computer, which will then provide organized offensive tendency information about an upcoming opponent. This form is complete with all the necessary information listed in the play diagram square and in the computer input section.

This form, although only page size (must be used in a full-sized notebook), has everything necessary to gather the scouting information and to transfer it to the computer. It should be used by a staff that is large enough to properly gather the information and use the results to full advantage.

In the fully computerized system of scouting, such as that represented by the form in Figure 10-3, the upcoming opponents may be cross-tendencied in innumerable ways including the following categories:

1. Field zone tendencies
2. Hash (boundary and field tendencies)
3. Down and distance tendencies
4. Formation tendencies
5. Man-in-motion tendencies
6. Point-of-attack tendencies
7. Play action tendencies
8. Ball carrier tendencies
9. Pass action tendencies
10. Pass receiver tendencies
11. Pass zone tendencies
12. Time tendencies (when applicable—at the end of half or end of game)

In recording the play by play, it is important for the Scouting Crew to be sure that all the pertinent information is recorded on each of the sheets. This will allow the information to be programmed to tendency and cross-tendency the opponent's offense in a manner that will leave little or nothing to chance in defensive game-plan preparation. Of course, not all the blanks on the play-by-play form must be filled in on each play. For example, if the play is a run, the blanks for pass zone, receiver and time (unless last two minutes in half or game) will not be filled in. Likewise, on a pass play, the running play blanks will remain unused.

In drawing running plays or pass routes, the Scout should be sure to show the correct point of attack or passing zone so this important information can be used properly in the computer.

Figure 10-4 shows a play-by-play diagraming card of the type which is used in many computerized scouting systems. Note that it is more thorough in information required than the form in Figure 10-3. (It is also smaller and easier to work with. The cards are kept in a small hard-backed flip-through note-book.) Notice the additional information categories which do not appear on the form in Figure 10-3:

1. Quarter of play
2. Ending yard line
3. More specific passing zones
4. Passer's number
5. Error (fumble, interception, etc.)
6. Penalties
7. Score

With this additional information, a much more complete program can be computed to give a more detailed look at the opponent's offense. Once again, this type of computer scouting system is one that should be used by a staff with adequate personnel to properly gather and use the information required to execute the system properly.

Figure 10-5 indicates the scouting form often used in a less complicated computerized scouting system. This type of form is used a great deal by medium and small size staffs which may not have the number of coaches or the experienced scouts to use the aforementioned systems, and yet, still desire to scout by the computer method.

Set up on a full-sized sheet, each form provides space for four plays (an entire four-down series). This form is very helpful when the Scouting Crew is small because more time can be spent writing and working, and less time flipping cards or pages. Also notice that much less information is required to complete each play-by-play segment. At the same time, all the pertinent information is called for which is necessary to program for the opponent's important offensive tendencies.

One well-organized Scout can adequately complete this form, and two Scouts can do an excellent and thorough job of scouting an opponent's offense using this method. Notice the stars beside several of the items on the right side of each play recording segment. The starred items must be filled in at the time the play takes place. The other items may be filled in later for the purpose of programming the computer.

The major difference between this form and Figures 10-3 and 10-4 is the manner in which the compiled information is recorded. Many staffs who use this method choose to copy the information from the computer read-out screen themselves, rather than having the information recorded on print-out sheets. This method is less costly than the completed print-out sheet method, and the staff has its choice of forms on which to record the information in this system.

The advantages of the multi-segmented sheet computer scouting method are

1. It is used by small and medium size staffs.
2. Scouting forms are less detailed with more play-by-play segments per page. (It is a much less complicated information-gathering system.)
3. It is used by staffs who have access to a computer through the school or through some other helpful organization.
4. It is more economical than fully computerized scouting methods.
5. The information gathered on the computer form can be assimilated in greater detail than by the staff on its own forms.
6. Smaller Scouting Crews can secure the necessary information.

## Full to Medium Staffs—Standard Scouting System

The full to medium size staff, using the standard scouting system, can almost tendency an offensive opponent as well as a computer can. The difference is that the staff (Scouts in particular) must do all the compilation themselves.

To accomplish this, the full or medium staff can use play-by-play cards much like the computerized card in Figure 10-4. The major difference is that the play-by-play cards in the standard system are themselves the tendency-determining materials.

As you can see in Figures 10-6 and 10-7, the play-by-play cards are less detailed in the play diagraming area. Also notice that they contain small holes in each information-gathering slot. These holes are the "computer" for the staff who uses the standard method of scouting. The holes are used along with a piece of small gauge wire.

This standard scouting method is accomplished in the following manner:

1. The Scout draws each offensive play, card by card, marking a check on the information slot which matches each situation. (Example: Figure 10-6. A check will be made in the appropriate slots to indicate: (1) first down, (2) 10 yards to go, (3) left hash, (4) free wheeling zone, (5) number 3 formation, (6) run, (7) ball carrier number 2, (8) +4 yards, (9) 2nd quarter, (10) time no factor, (11) play number 32.)
2. In Figure 10-7, a similar process is followed, with the extra information recorded as called for by the play-by-play card.
3. Before the Scouts begin their compilation work, they clip out each slot marked on each card with a wedged paper clipper or punch.
4. Now, each card is already automatically tendencied.
5. Then the Scout stacks the cards, which have been color-coded by games. (By coloring the card ends with a different color for each game, and by numbering the cards, they can be reassembled in order after tendencying.) The Scout then runs a small wire (may be from a coat hanger) through each slot hole in the order in which he wants the information.
6. Each card clipped in the slot that the Scout runs the wire through will fall out when shaken. All the cards which fall out are noted, and tendencies are formed in this manner.

More information on this compilation method is contained in Chapter 15.

As you can see, strong tendencies can be uncovered by this standard scouting method. Combined with film study, this scouting method will provide more than ample information for an excellent game plan by a defensive staff.

### Limited Staffs—Standard Scouting System

It should be mentioned here that a small staff size should not limit a Head Coach to any particular scouting system. If there is an excellent Scout on a small staff, a computerized system or a more sophisticated standard system than that outlined below may be used. The purpose of this section is to aid the small staff who needs simple, yet thorough, methods of securing the necessary play-by-play information to meet its requirements. This staff may have only one person free to scout upcoming opponents. This person may be a totally inexperienced young coach or he may be the team's student manager.

Whatever the situation is, the play-by-play information-gathering forms discussed here will be very basic in nature. (If more information is necessary for your staff, add the desired categories from the previously discussed information-gathering forms.) The forms depicted in Figures 10-8 and 10-9 require only the most simple information with respect to play-by-play recording. Figure 10-8 shows a play-by-play card used for gathering only the most basic information about the upcoming opponent's offensive attack. Categories called for are

1. Hash
2. Field spot (This is marked by arrowhead, >, on the approximate yard line on the scale provided. The arrowhead should point in the direction the offense is moving. This spot marking method saves time.)
3. Down
4. Distance
5. Play diagram
6. Gain or loss
7. Remarks (This category will be expanded upon as the Scout becomes more adept in gathering the offensive information. Much valuable information can be secured by using the "Remarks" spaces during each game.)

This simplified card system is an excellent method for the single Scout who must gather the necessary offensive information. However, having to flip the cards after each play can be a problem for the Scout who is working alone. For those Scouts who are bothered by having to flip cards each play, Figure 10-9 illustrates a full sheet play-by-play information-gathering form. This form contains eight play recording segments, representing two full four-play series which may be recorded on each sheet.

Also, the information called for is even less than that required on the card in Figure 10-8. Notice that only the following information is called for:

1. Down
2. Distance
3. Field position
4. Play diagram
5. Remarks (if time)

This is such a simple form that the Head Coach who works alone or a Staff of one can send his student manager or trainer to scout an upcoming opponent and get some valuable help from the report. It is also an excellent form to use for

1. Training new coaches to scout;
2. Young or inexperienced scouts working a game alone;
3. Formation tendencying of an opponent while compiling scouting information
4. Recording upcoming opponent's offense from films. The point to be made here is that the preceding offensive scouting forms are not the only good information-gathering systems. By studying these various systems, however, an imaginative coach can do wonders in upgrading and improving his present system by combining and rearranging ideas.

## Recording Play by Play from Film

On many staffs, the only scout report available comes from viewing films of the upcoming opponent. This form of scouting has many drawbacks, but can also provide adequate information about the upcoming opponent's offense.

Figure 10-10 illustrates an excellent form on which to record the upcoming opponent's offense from film. With three play segments on each sheet, the offense can be followed in sequence easily and there is less paper shuffling than with "one play" cards. This form asks for the following material:

1. Down
2. Distance
3. Hash
4. Yard line (+ or − system)
5. Play diagram
6. Yards gained

If more information is desired, it can be taken easily from the film by studying it several times. The scouting form in Figure 10-9 is also good to use for taking play-by-play offensive information from opponent's films.

Some coaches also like to chart the film as well as collect the play-by-play diagrams. Figure 10-11 depicts a typical film charting form which keeps the upcoming opponent's offensive attack in perspective with respect to chronology. Similar forms are used to verify the play-by-play information brought back by the Scouting Crew. (This is, of course, when the Scouting Crew has scouted the same game which you have on film.)

Whether the staff uses film as the scouting source or whether film is the source for confirmation of the Scouting Crew's work, much useful information can be gained from film study. Some examples are

1. Exact alignment by formation;
2. Line blocking patterns (particularly trap, double team, cross block, pull and lead, fold, hinge, etc.);
3. Exactness of pass routes of all receivers (in most cases);
4. Exact point of attack on running plays;
5. Unusual individual mannerisms of players which may be used as tip-offs;
6. All the aforementioned tendency charts and forms can be completed for the tendencying process.

## Recording Play by Play with a Code System

Another increasingly popular system of recording play by play is the code method. In this system, the Scouts use a written code to record each play, rather than drawing the offensive action. This recording system is particularly effective if a film of the game scouted is available. This method is also especially good with respect to ease of recording and the time element involved in putting each play on paper.

Following are two examples of code which can be used instead of drawing play by play:

| Word-Letter System | | |
|---|---|---|
| Formation | Play | Ball Carrier |
| PR (Pro Right) | Op.R (Option Right) | g (give) |

Using this system then, PR; OP.R; g would represent a Pro Right formation, the play being the Base Option to the Right with the ball given to the right half back.

| Number System | | |
|---|---|---|
| Formation | Play | Ball Carrier |
| #1 (Pro Right) | 34 (Base Option Right) | 2 (Right Half) |

In this system, #1; 34; 2 represents the same play as described in the Word-Letter System above. (Backs are numbered: QB = #1, RH = #2, LH = #3, FI or WB = #4). By numbering the formations in the order they appear in the game, the plays by series and the backs as shown, the number play-by-play system is a very simple way of recording the upcoming opponent's offense. Other ideas for codes to be used in written play-by-play recording systems may be found in Figure 10-3. Any code system devised which meets the Coach's needs will do nicely.

The other basic information such as down-distance, hash, and yardage gained can remain the same in this system as in the play drawing systems. An excellent form for the written code system of recording is shown in Figure 10-11. The Coach may wish to alter this form to fit his own situation. This system also blends well into any type of computerized scouting system. The code can easily be transferred into the terminal without having to re-record pre-drawn play by play.

## STRENGTHS AND WEAKNESSES

The value of knowing the strengths and weaknesses of the upcoming opponent's offense cannot be emphasized enough. This is particularly true when the opponents show very few tangible tendencies. (Often, teams scout themselves in various ways to be sure they are not setting offensive tendencies.) In other words, most teams work hard not to develop tendencies which can be capitalized upon by their opponents.

When an upcoming opponent who is being scouted sets very few tendencies, the importance of their strengths and weaknesses become much greater than normal. For example, if a team is as likely to throw on first down as it is to run, and as likely to run on third and long as it is to pass, you had better know the basic strengths and weaknesses of that team very well.

If a team sets few tendencies, it is imperative that a staff know what must be stopped in 1, 2, 3, order, and be ready to stop these best plays on every down. To know this, three areas of the upcoming opponent's offense must be well scouted: (1) offensive style strengths and weaknesses; (2) team personnel strengths and weaknesses and; (3) individual strengths and weaknesses.

### Team Offensive Style

The opponent's offensive style will indicate strengths and weaknesses. For example, a team which uses a power running game is likely to be strong in areas of the blast play, power sweep, trap, and off tackle power. Very likely, the same team will be rather weak in terms of a sophisticated drop back passing game. Knowing this is very important to the Defensive Coordinator in forming the game plan.

It is a high priority for the Scouting Crew to determine the strengths and weaknesses of an upcoming opponent's offensive style. The strengths should be outlined and detailed in 1, 2, 3 fashion and thoroughly explained to the staff. Weaknesses should be handled in the same manner so the staff can plan to exploit these areas.

## Team Personnel

Team personnel strengths and weaknesses should also be detected and reported to the staff. For example, overall offensive team speed or lack of it is an important category for the Defensive Coordinator to be familiar with in preparing the game plan for upcoming opponents. Any other offensive team personnel idiosyncracies displayed by the opponents should be recorded by the Scouting Crew and reported to the staff.

## Individual Personnel

Possibly, the single most important phase of scouting is to accurately gauge the abilities and inabilities of each individual offensive player for the upcoming opponents. For instance, all the tendencies in the world are not worth knowing that the opponent's "I" tailback is their only outstanding offensive player and that the quarterback throws very poorly if pressured at all. Knowing these facts, the Defensive Coordinator can set his plan accordingly. Add familiarities of opponent's tendencies to this individual personnel knowledge, and a very strong defensive game plan can be formed. Pick up, record and transfer to the staff every tidbit possible about the opponent's offensive personnel.

## Tip-Offs

The Scouting Crew should record and report anything special that the opponents do, teamwise or individually, that may be used as a tip-off for the defensive unit. Knowing when a particular play or maneuver is coming will be very valuable to the defense.

## WRAP-UP

Remember that the most important thing in the process of gathering offensive scouting information concerning an opponent is to be sure to answer accurately the question, "What Must We Stop?" All phases of scouting should be directed toward this end.

Also remember that the type of system, whether computerized or standard, is not as important as what that system delivers in information which is compatible and usable to your football program. There are many ways in which computerized scouting can be instituted, and it is not as complicated as one might think. Also, the staff that either does not want or cannot afford the computerized method should remember that standardized scouting can be just as effective if enough effort is expended in the proper preparation of the system itself, regardless of staff size.

It should also be mentioned here that only the scouting methods and forms were discussed in this chapter. Compilation methods (including programming computer input) and forms will be discussed in Chapter 14.

OFFENSIVE PERSONNEL

Opponent Scouted________________ Date ____________

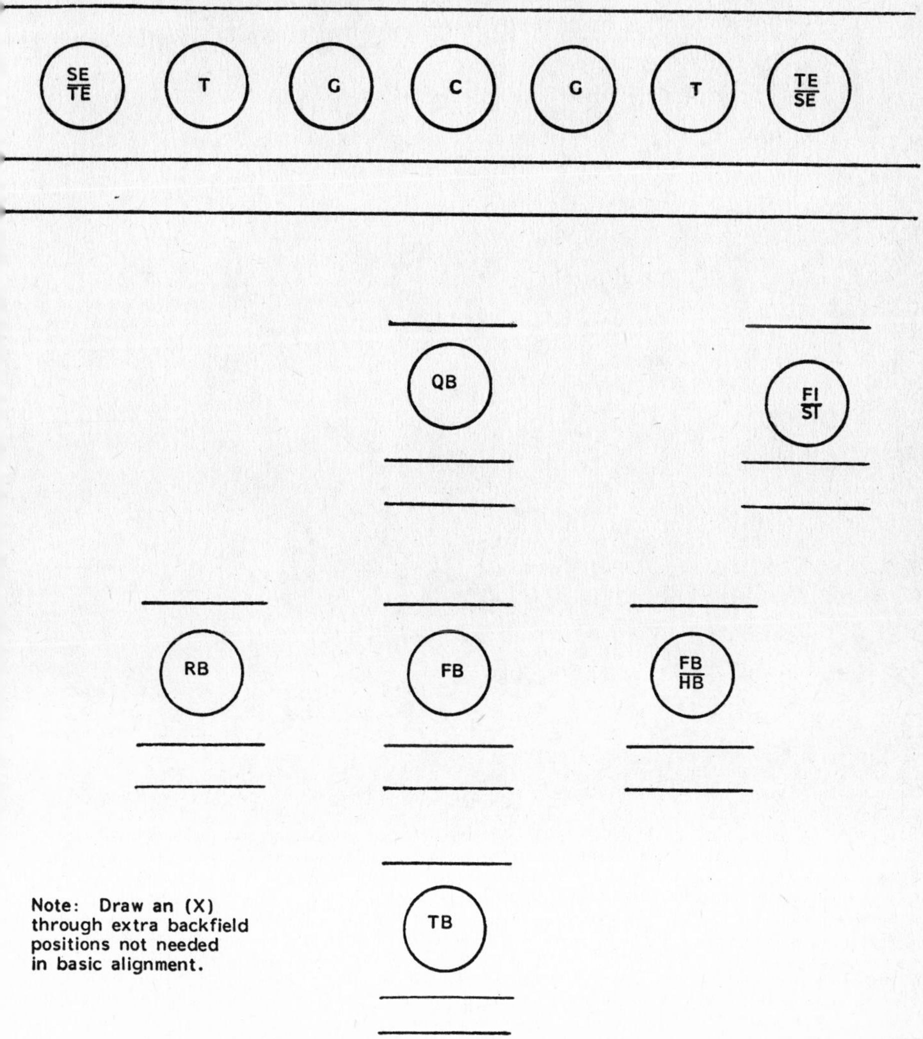
SE/TE
T
G
C
G
T
TE/SE
QB
FI/ST
RB
FB
FB/HB
TB
Note: Draw an (X) through extra backfield positions not needed in basic alignment.

Figure 10-1

**KEY MAN IN BASIC FORMATIONS**

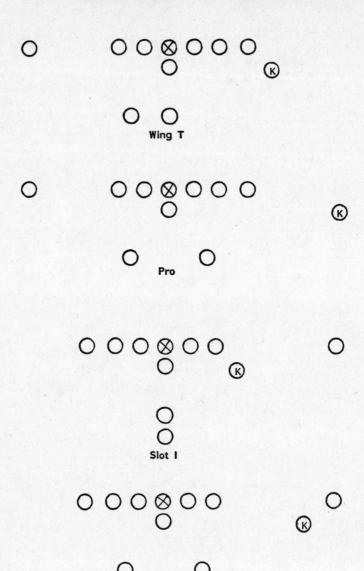

Wing T

Pro

Slot I

Twins

Figure 10-2

COMPUTER SCOUTING SHEET

**Yard Line:** 1-10 ○  11-25 ○  26-50 ○  49-26 ○  25-11 ○  10-5 ○  4-1 ○

**Hash:** L ○  M ○  R ○

**Down:** 1 ○  2 ○  3 ○  4 ○

**Distance:** 15+ ○  11-15 ○  10 ○  6-9 ○  3-5 ○  1-2 ○

**Formation (Describe):** 1 ○  2 ○  3 ○  4 ○  5 ○  6 ○  7 ○  8 ○  9 ○  10 ○  11 ○  12 ○  13 ○  14 ○

**Motion:** FI cross ○  FI away ○  SI cross ○  SI away ○  RB strong ○  RB weak ○  FB strong ○  FB weak ○  TB strong ○  TB weak ○  QB strong ○  QB weak ○

**Type Play:** Run ○  Pass ○  Punt ○  Field Goal ○  Extra Point ○

**Gain:** 0 ○  1-4 ○  5-7 ○  8-10 ○  11-14 ○  15-17 ○  18-25 ○  26-35 ○  36-45 ○  46&Up ○

**Loss:** 1 to 4 ○  5 to 7 ○  8 to 10 ○  11 & Up ○

**Other:** Inc. ○  Inter. ○  Fum. ○  Pen. ○

**P of A:** 9 ○  7 ○  5 ○  3 ○  1 ○  0 ○  2 ○  4 ○  6 ○  8 ○

**Zone:** 1 ○  2 ○  3 ○  4 ○  5 ○  6 ○  7 ○  8 ○  9 ○

**Play Action:** Inside Opt. ○  Outside Opt. ○  Load ○  Counter ○  Counter Opt. ○  Trap ○  Trap Opt. ○  Blast ○  Lead Dr. ○  D.B. Dr. ○  Bootleg R. ○  Reverse ○

**Yd Ln___ Hash___:** 1 ○  2 ○  3 ○  4 ○  5 ○

**Dn___ Dis___:** 6 ○ 11 ○  7 ○ 12 ○  8 ○ 13 ○  9 ○ 14 ○  10 ○ 15 ○

**Gain___ Loss___:** 16 ○  17 ○  18 ○  19 ○  20 ○

**P of A___ Zone___:** 21 ○ 26 ○  22 ○ 27 ○  23 ○ 28 ○  24 ○ 29 ○  25 ○ 30 ○

**BC___ Rec___:** 31 ○  32 ○  33 ○  34 ○  35 ○

**Play #___ Time___:** 36 ○  37 ○  38 ○  39 ○  40 ○

**Ball Carrier:** RB #1 ○  RB #2 ○  FB #1 ○  FB #2 ○  QB #1 ○  QB #2 ○  FI #1 ○  FI #2 ○  SI #1 ○  SI #2 ○  Other ○

**Pass Action:** Drop B. ○  Sprint ○  Play Act. ○  Bootleg P. ○  Mid. Scr. ○  9 Scr. ○  8 Scr. ○  Sweep P. ○  Other ○

**Pass Receiver:** SE #1 ○  SE #2 ○  FI #1 ○  FI #2 ○  TE #1 ○  TE #2 ○  RB #1 ○  RB #2 ○  FB #1 ○  FB #2 ○  QB #1 ○

Field diagram grid numbered 1 through 9 with offensive alignment marks (○ and ⊗).

Figure 10-3

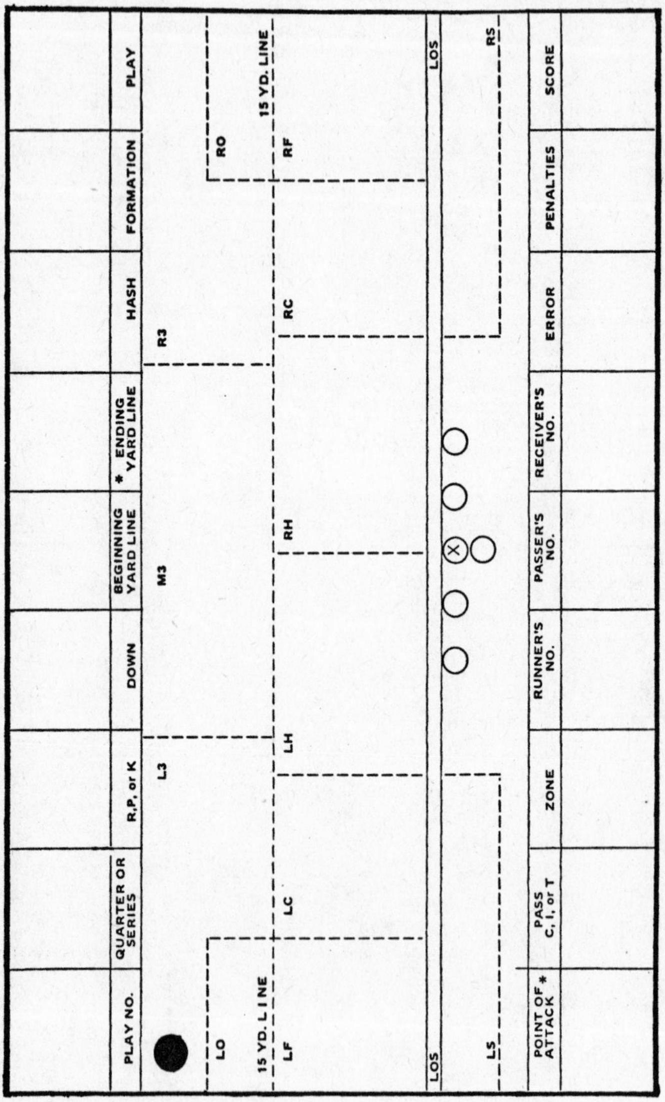

Figure 10-4

COMPUTER PLAY-BY-PLAY MULTI-SHEET

| 1 | 2 | 3 | *HASH |
|---|---|---|---|
| | | | *YD LINE |
| | | | *DOWN |

| 4 | 5 | 6 | 7 | 8 | *DISTANCE |
|---|---|---|---|---|---|
| | | | | | FORMATION |
| | | | | | PLAY |
| | | | | | *PLAYER |
| | | | | | *RESULT |
| | | | | | HOLE/ZONE |
| | | | | | TYPE |

| 1 | 2 | 3 | *HASH |
|---|---|---|---|
| | | | *YD LINE |
| | | | *DOWN |

| 4 | 5 | 6 | 7 | 8 | *DISTANCE |
|---|---|---|---|---|---|
| | | | | | FORMATION |
| | | | | | PLAY |
| | | | | | *PLAYER |
| | | | | | *RESULT |
| | | | | | HOLE/ZONE |
| | | | | | TYPE |

| 1 | 2 | 3 | *HASH |
|---|---|---|---|
| | | | *YD LINE |
| | | | *DOWN |

| 4 | 5 | 6 | 7 | 8 | *DISTANCE |
|---|---|---|---|---|---|
| | | | | | FORMATION |
| | | | | | PLAY |
| | | | | | *PLAYER |
| | | | | | *RESULT |
| | | | | | HOLE/ZONE |
| | | | | | TYPE |

| 1 | 2 | 3 | *HASH |
|---|---|---|---|
| | | | *YD LINE |
| | | | *DOWN |

| 4 | 5 | 6 | 7 | 8 | *DISTANCE |
|---|---|---|---|---|---|
| | | | | | FORMATION |
| | | | | | PLAY |
| | | | | | *PLAYER |
| | | | | | *RESULT |
| | | | | | HOLE/ZONE |
| | | | | | TYPE |

Figure 10-5

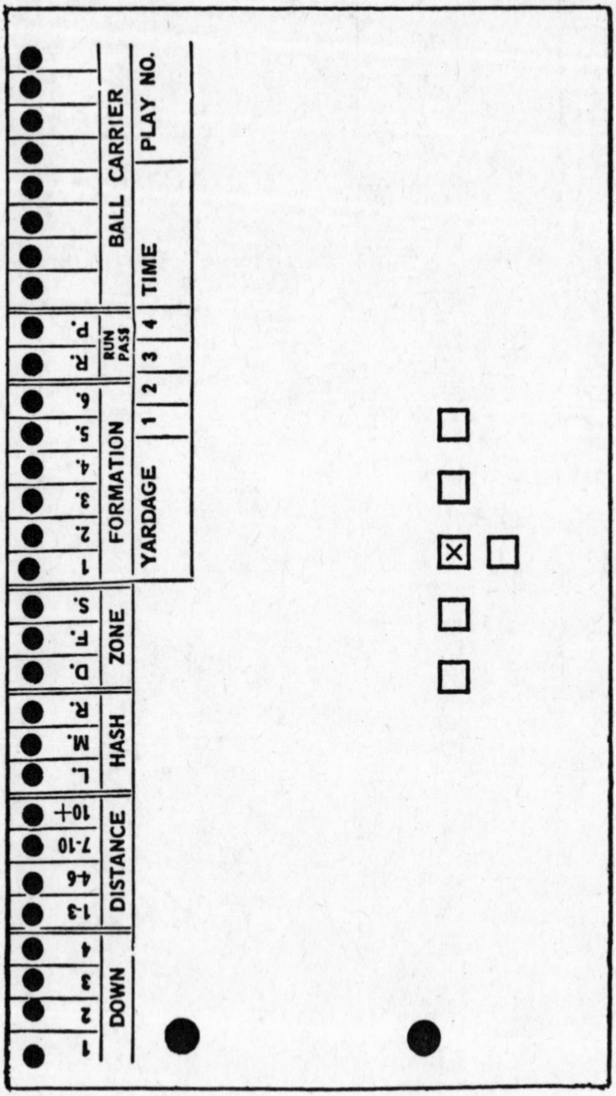

Figure 10-6

COMPLETE STANDARD PLAY-BY-PLAY CARD

Tendency — Short Side, Wide Side, Weak Side, Strong Side

Crucial Play

Ball Carrier or Intended Receiver — 1 2 3 4 5 6 7 8 9 10

Pass Play

Formation — 1 2 3 4 5 6 7 8 9 10

Distance — 1-3 4-6 7-10 10+

Down — 1 2 3 4

Hash — L M R

Territory — :: - + ++

QUARTER TIME LEFT

GAIN

CARD #

Figure 10-7

LIMITED STANDARD PLAY-BY-PLAY CARD

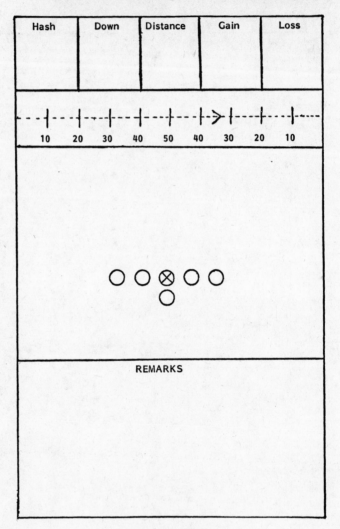

Figure 10-8

LIMITED PLAY-BY-PLAY SHEET

○ ○ ⊗ ○ ○
○

Dn.___  Dist._____  F.P._____  _____
Remarks:

○ ○ ⊗ ○ ○
○

Dn.___  Dist._____  F.P._____  _____
Remarks:

○ ○ ⊗ ○ ○
○

Dn.___  Dist._____  F.P._____  _____
Remarks:

○ ○ ⊗ ○ ○
○

Dn.___  Dist._____  F.P._____  _____
Remarks:

○ ○ ⊗ ○ ○
○

Dn.___  Dist._____  F.P._____  _____
Remarks:

○ ○ ⊗ ○ ○
○

Dn.___  Dist._____  F.P._____  _____
Remarks:

○ ○ ⊗ ○ ○
○

Dn.___  Dist._____  F.P._____  _____
Remarks:

○ ○ ⊗ ○ ○
○

Dn.___  Dist._____  F.P._____  _____
Remarks:

Figure 10-9

FILM SCOUTING FORM

TEAM_____            DATE_____

---

| DOWN | DISTANCE | HASH | YARD LINE |
|------|----------|------|-----------|
| 1 2 3 4 | 1 2 3 4 5 6 7 8 9 10+ | L M R | _____ |

YARDS GAINED

_____

○ ○ ⊗ ○ ○
○

REMARKS

---

| DOWN | DISTANCE | HASH | YARD LINE |
|------|----------|------|-----------|
| 1 2 3 4 | 1 2 3 4 5 6 7 8 9 10+ | L M R | _____ |

YARDS GAINED

_____

○ ○ ⊗ ○ ○
○

REMARKS

---

| DOWN | DISTANCE | HASH | YARD LINE |
|------|----------|------|-----------|
| 1 2 3 4 | 1 2 3 4 5 6 7 8 9 10+ | L M R | _____ |

YARDS GAINED

_____

○ ○ ⊗ ○ ○
○

REMARKS

---

OTHER INFORMATION

Figure 10-10

**FILM CHARTING FORM**

| Play No. | Yd. Line | Hash | Down | Dist. | Off. Set | Play | Remark |
|----------|----------|------|------|-------|----------|------|--------|
| 1 | | | | | | | |
| 2 | | | | | | | |
| 3 | | | | | | | |
| 4 | | | | | | | |
| 5 | | | | | | | |
| 6 | | | | | | | |
| 7 | | | | | | | |
| 8 | | | | | | | |
| 9 | | | | | | | |
| 10 | | | | | | | |
| 11 | | | | | | | |
| 12 | | | | | | | |
| 13 | | | | | | | |
| 14 | | | | | | | |
| 15 | | | | | | | |
| 16 | | | | | | | |
| 17 | | | | | | | |
| 18 | | | | | | | |
| 19 | | | | | | | |
| 20 | | | | | | | |
| 21 | | | | | | | |
| 22 | | | | | | | |
| 23 | | | | | | | |
| 24 | | | | | | | |

Figure 10-11

# 11

# HOW TO SCOUT THE DEFENSE
## (Staff and Scouts)

BECAUSE football defense depends basically upon reaction to offensive maneuvers, it is often much harder to scout than offense. Add to this the complexities of various defensive adjustments, stunts, slants, specialized secondary coverages, and the Scouts have to be consistently on their toes to scout the opponent's defense accurately. This is particularly true if film of the opponents is not available.

## DEFENSIVE PERSONNEL

### Defensive Starters

As was mentioned in Chapter 9, if the opponents go through any team defensive drills in pre-game warm-up, a tentative knowledge of their starting lineup may be acquired before the game begins. (Refer to Figure 7-5 in Chapter 7 for an example of a defensive personnel recording instrument.) If the opponents hold no team defensive pre-game drills, the Scouts should secure the starting defensive lineup during the opponent's first series on defense.

If the opponents are being scouted for the first time by your staff, it is very important to get every player in his correct position. If the opponents have been scouted by you previously, the Scouts should note any personnel changes from earlier games and try to find out the reasons for the changes.

## Replacements

Substitutions play a major role in many teams' specialized situation defenses today. Your Scouts should be very
alert to the replacement of starters. The game situations at the
time of substitutions and the resulting defensive alignment
should be carefully noted. Substituting an extra defensive back
in a passing situation or substituting a defensive lineman for a
secondary player on a short-yardage play will set definite
tendencies which should be noted closely.

In addition to making sure to get the correct jersey
numbers of all replacements, the Scouts should also attempt to
gain every bit of insight into the reasons for the replacements,
noting the abilities of the replacements and any other specifics
that are possible concerning substitutions.

## Flip-Flop or Stationary Positioning

The flip-flopping of at least part of the defensive personnel according to offensive strength is a popular trend today.
Most teams flip the linebackers and the safeties. Others also
flip the entire secondary, and still others flip the defensive
ends.

In scouting an opponent's defense, the Scouts must
quickly pick up any flip-flopping of personnel if this practice
seems to be part of the defensive pattern. Some teams flip-flop
no one, leaving its personnel in a stationary right-left side
alignment. Whatever the personnel placement, the Scouts
should note all the specifics, particularly any strengths or
weaknesses inherent in the opponent's personnel placement.

## RECORDING DEFENSIVE PLAY BY PLAY

Since most defenses today are multiple to some degree
and therefore, complex, probably the best way to record
defensive play by play is through the use of a simple instrument. Figure 11-1 illustrates such an instrument, which allows
the Scouts to record the general defensive information rapidly
and also allows time between plays for drawing and working

on the opponent's specific defensive maneuvers a little at a time.

This form allows a defensive analysis of the opponents from the following standpoints:

1. Down and distance
2. Position on the field
3. Right and left side defensive front alignments (if multiple)
4. Defensive strengths or weaknesses by point of attack
5. Passing success versus secondary

Also, notations can be made in the secondary columns concerning secondary coverages, etc., and if hash tendencies are desired, simply add an L, M or R to the yard line number in the second column.

If more specific information is desired on the secondary as to coverages according to field position, Figure 11-2 shows an excellent, simple chart which will yield such results about the opponent's secondary.

There are, of course, many other ways to record defensive play by play. The key is to keep the recording instruments very simple so that the Scouts will have time to draw and detail the specific maneuvers of the opponents as changes and adjustments are made.

## OPPONENT'S DEFENSIVE ALIGNMENTS

A very integral part of scouting the opponent's defense is the recording of their various defensive front and secondary alignments and the reaction from each. (In situations where film of the game being scouted is not available or if the game is being worked by only one Scout, the drawing of the opponent's defensive alignments may be more important and may provide more pertinent information than using a play-by-play recording chart.)

### Recording Defensive Front Alignments

An excellent form for recording defensive front alignments is shown in Figure 11-3. While recording the opponent's front alignments, the Scouts should carefully scrutinize each maneuver and be very specific in putting the information on paper. Following are some of the important factors which should be recorded concerning defensive front alignments:

1. *Basic Alignment*

   (a)  Personnel (jersey numbers, capabilities, flip-flop, etc.)
   (b)  Exact alignments (example: Left tackle-5 technique)
   (c)  Reaction (example: Left tackle—delivers inside forearm, high, soft charge)
   (d)  Anything outstanding or unusual

(Draw the basic front set including linebackers very specifically.)

2. *Other Sets or Adjustments*

   (a)  Any other normal sets
   (b)  Adjustments of basic alignments
   (c)  Reactions from these sets or adjustments
   (d)  Unit slants or loops

3. *Stunts or Games*

   (a)  Diagram all stunts specifically
   (b)  Any tip-offs that give away stunts

4. *Goal Line or Short-Yardage Alignments*

   (a)  Exact alignment of front personnel
   (b)  Exact charge of down men
   (c)  Blitz or run-through by linebackers or secondary
   (d)  Responsibilities of off-tackle and outside personnel

5. *Prevent Alignment*

   (a)  Exact alignment
   (b)  Who rushes—who has draw—who has screens
   (c)  Best pass rusher

## Recording Secondary Alignments and Coverages

Figure 11-4 depicts a secondary alignment and coverage recording form for diagraming specific maneuvers by the opponents.

Secondary play has become much more multiple and complex in recent years. For this reason, your Scouts must be diligent in securing all important information concerning the opponent's secondary play.

### 1. Basic Secondary Alignment

(a)  Personnel (jersey numbers, ability, flip-flop)
(b)  Type coverage (two-deep, three-deep, invert, roll, etc.)
(c)  Depths of personnel and alignment
(d)  Zone or man-to-man
(e)  Reactions
(f)  Anything outstanding or unusual

### 2. Other Coverages or Adjustments

(a)  Any other coverages
(b)  Adjustments of basic coverage
(c)  Reactions from other coverages
(d)  Bump or chug receivers
(e)  Full roll (strong or weak)

### 3. Secondary Stunts or Variations

(a)  Safety blitz
(b)  Corner stunts
(c)  Combination man-to-man and zone

### 4. Goal Line or Short-Yardage Coverage

(a)  Man-to-man or zone
(b)  Responsibilities of personnel
(c)  Speed of reaction to run or run fake
(d)  Blitz or corner stunts

### 5. Prevent or Long-Yardage Coverage

(a)  Any change in personnel
(b)  Two- deep or three- deep
(c)  Underneath coverage
(d)  Man-to-man or zone
(e)  Reaction to support run

## DEFENSIVE STRENGTHS AND WEAKNESSES

The Scouting Crew, as it is working the opponent's defense, should look beyond the alignments and coverages into the depths of the opponent's defensive scheme and theory, particularly those relating to personnel.

### Defensive Style

Every defense has some inherent weakness. For example, a gapping or hard-charging front wall should be susceptible to traps, draws and screens. Teams which play soft front techniques will have good pursuit, but are not usually strong against quick-hitting plays or the inside power game.

A straight three-deep secondary has problems defensing the run and pass in option attacks and with flood routes in the passing game. Two-deep secondaries have weaknesses in covering quick, deep and medium routes, but are usually very strong against the outside run.

There are many other examples of every basic defense's strengths and weaknesses. What the Scouts are interested in is finding out information about the opponent's basic alignment, particularly which things can be used to advantage by the Varsity offensive unit.

### Team Personnel

Team personnel traits such as above-average team speed or lack of it, quickness in reaction, size, and other group capabilities should be noted. Often, well-diagnosed findings in these areas can be as important as any of the other information secured by the Scouting Crew.

### Individual Personnel

This category is a most important phase of the Scouts' work in scouting the opponent's defense. A great deal of effort should be put into breaking down the opponent's defensive unit one player at a time with respect to individual strengths and weaknesses. In doing so, the Scouts are likely to discover several possibilities for attack plans, which may be used by the Varsity Staff in preparing for the opponent's defense.

Players who can be run straight at; others who must be double-teamed; those who pursue too rapidly; a secondary player who can be beat deep off of a good running play fake, are all examples of important individual personnel strengths and weaknesses which should be noted very specifically by the Scouts. There are, of course, many other strengths and weaknesses of an individual nature which will be very helpful, and even the most minute of these should be recorded by the Scouts.

### Tip-Offs

The Scouting Crew should be very alert to any tip-offs which the opponents may give that may help determine when specific defensive maneuvers may be coming. For example, the opponents may tip off stunts by the alignment of one or several players prior to the snap. Or a secondary maneuver, such as a safety blitz or a full roll to one side or the other on the snap, may be tipped off by the mannerisms of one or more of the players involved. Whatever the tip-offs are, the Scouts should pay particular attention to them and record them accordingly.

## WRAP-UP

As was mentioned earlier, the inherent nature of defense (reacting to offensive maneuvers) make the scouting of this phase of the game somewhat different. For this reason, this chapter included many less forms for recording the defense than, for example, the preceding chapter contained for scouting the offense. The reason is that the scouting of defense is more individual and unit-oriented and therefore, the procedure of collecting information is not nearly so important as is the correct understanding of what the opponents are doing defensively, the situations in which they make changes, and the exact alignments and depths of their personnel in the various defensive sets used.

To sum up the scouting of the opponent's defense, Scouts should continuously remember that the entire process should be carried out with "Where Can We Move It?" at the heart of all work done. A thorough scouting job on the opponent's defense will provide the answers to this important question.

DEFENSIVE PLAY-BY-PLAY CHART

Opponent Scouted_____

| Down & Distance | Yard Line | Defense L.        R. | 9 | 7 | 5 | 3 | 0 | 2 | 4 | 6 | 8 | Passing Zone Results & Distance |
|---|---|---|---|---|---|---|---|---|---|---|---|---|
| | + − | | | | | | | | | | | |
| | + − | | | | | | | | | | | |
| | + − | | | | | | | | | | | |
| | + − | | | | | | | | | | | |
| | + − | | | | | | | | | | | |
| | + − | | | | | | | | | | | |
| | + − | | | | | | | | | | | |
| | + − | | | | | | | | | | | |
| | + − | | | | | | | | | | | |
| | + − | | | | | | | | | | | |
| | + − | | | | | | | | | | | |
| | + − | | | | | | | | | | | |
| | + − | | | | | | | | | | | |
| | + − | | | | | | | | | | | |
| | + − | | | | | | | | | | | |
| | + − | | | | | | | | | | | |
| | + − | | | | | | | | | | | |

Figure 11-1

## SECONDARY HASH TENDENCY CHART

Opponent Scouted_____

(Indicate type coverage used in each sequence)

| LEFT HASH | | | RIGHT HASH | | |
|---|---|---|---|---|---|
| Short Side | | Wide Side | Wide Side | Short Side | |
| Roll | Invert | | | Roll | Invert |
| | | | | | |
| | | | | | |
| | | | | | |
| | | | | | |
| | | | | | |
| | | | | | |
| | | | | | |
| | | | | | |
| | | | | | |
| | | | | | |
| | | | | | |
| | | | | | |
| | | | | | |
| | | | | | |
| | | | | | |
| | | | | | |
| | | | | | |
| | | | | | |
| | | | | | |
| | | | | | |
| | | | | | |
| | | | | | |
| | | | | | |
| | | | | | |
| | | | | | |

Figure 11-2

DEFENSIVE FRONT ALIGNMENT SHEET

Opponent Scouted_____

1. Basic Front Alignment (Be specific about individual alignments and list numbers)

| 2. Other Sets or Adjustments | 3. Other Sets or Adjustments |
|---|---|
| 4. Stunts or Games | 5. Stunts or Games |
| 6. Goal Line - Short Yardage | 7. Prevent - Long Yardage |

Figure 11-3

DEFENSIVE SECONDARY COVERAGE SHEET

Opponent Scouted_____

1. Basic Secondary Alignment (list players' numbers and describe zone, man, etc.)

| 2. Other Coverages or Adjustments | 3. Other Coverages or Adjustments |
|---|---|
| 4. Secondary Stunts or Variations | 5. Secondary Stunts or Variations |
| 6. Goal Line - Short Yardage Coverage | 7. Prevent Coverage |

Figure 11-4

# 12

# HOW TO SCOUT THE KICKING GAME
## (Staff and Scouts)

THE kicking game—all phases—can win or lose as many or more games as the offense or defense can. Wise coaches spend a good portion of their preparation and workout time working on the kicking game. Scouts should also be prepared to do a very thorough job of scouting the opponent's kicking game. This will allow the Varsity Staff to be completely prepared in this most vital area.

## THE PUNTING GAME

Of the different kicking game phases, the punt and punt return are normally the most frequently used, and both can change the complexion of a game very quickly. Scouting the punting game should rate a high priority, right alongside and as part of, the offense and defense. Figure 12-1 illustrates a sheet for recording particulars about the punting game.

### The Punt Team

In scouting the opponent's punt team, Scouts should pay particular attention to, and be specific in, the recording of the following items:

1. *Basic punting alignment (jersey numbers)*

(a) Line splits
(b) Up backs and personal protector or three- across punter protection?
(c) Depth of punter
(d) Any personnel split away from the formation?

2. *Punt mechanics and blocking*

(a) Time from snap to punt (stopwatch)
(b) Hang time and normal zone kicked in (L-M-R)
(c) Type blocking for punter
(d) Length of blocks before coverage begins. Linemen? Blocking backs?

3. *Punt coverage (jersey numbers)*

(a) First man or men down
(b) Cover in waves? Any continual holes in coverage?
(c) Who are safeties? Do they use single safety?
(d) Do the outside contain men secure corner well? If not, which one?

4. *Punt team general information*

(a) Accuracy of center snap? Consistency?
(b) Steps taken by punter before contact with ball
(c) Holes or weak areas in punt team's blocking
(d) Does personal protector move out of position? Back up toward punter?
(e) Suggested areas for our attempts to block punt
(f) Suggested side for our punt return wall
(g) Do they run or pass from punt formation? Diagram.
(h) What type of punt formation do they use inside their 5-yard line?
(i) Do they quick kick? Who kicks? Can we block it?

## The Punt Return Team

These items should be recorded by the Scouts concerning the opponent's punt return team:

### 1. Punt return alignment

(a)  Defensive front (include linebackers)
(b)  Secondary return setup (jersey numbers)
(c)  Punt block alignment

### 2. Punt return mechanics

(a)  Wall return (left, right, both?)
(b)  Middle return (cross block?)
(c)  If two-deep, do they hand off or fake hand off? Is there an upback for fair catch?
(d)  Do they force punter from side away from wall only or from both sides?
(e)  Do they double team ends? Kick ends out or in to start return?

### 3. Punt block mechanics

(a)  What type or types punt block do they attempt? (middle, outside, etc.)
(b)  Does one particular player attempt to block all punts?
(c)  How many backs are in position to field punt if not blocked? How far is each from L.O.S.?
(d)  Do they fair catch if punt is not blocked, or try to return?

### 4. Punt return general information

(a)  Can we run or pass on their punt return alignment? Where? How?
(b)  Do they tip their return? How?
(c)  Do they tip their punt block attempts? How?
(d)  Do all return men have good hands? If not, who? (jersey number)
(e)  Any personnel change from return to block attempt? Who? Where in lineup?
(f)  Is their return dangerous enough that we should kick out of bounds?
(g)  Any other vital punt return information?

## THE KICKOFF GAME

Close scouting of the opponent's kickoff game can pay big dividends. (It should be mentioned here that except for the jersey numbers of the skilled people involved, it is much more important to record the actions of the opponent's kicking or receiving team than it is to get the number of every player on the line, etc. This is particularly true in the case of a limited staff Scouting Crew, especially if one Scout is working alone.)

Figure 12-2 shows an example of a kickoff game-recording sheet.

## The Kickoff Team

### 1. Kickoff team alignment

(a) Basic alignment (jersey numbers, if time)
(b) Ball in middle or on one hash? If on hash, which one?
(c) Type kicker—Conventional? Soccer?
(d) Onsides alignment?

### 2. Kickoff mechanics

(a) Height of kick and hang time (stopwatch)
(b) Normal depth of kick
(c) Does kicker kick away from best return man? If not, does he kick consistently into L, M, R?
(d) What type onsides kick? Where does kicker kick onsides?

### 3. Kickoff coverage (jersey numbers, if time)

(a) Do they stay in lanes?
(b) Do they cover straight down or do some players criss-cross? If they criss-cross, which players? Any holes? Where?
(c) Do they cover in waves or all come down together? Any holes? Where?
(d) Who is first player or players to ball?
(e) Which players contain the sidelines?
(f) Who is the safety or safeties?
(g) Show method used to attempt to recover onsides kick

### 4. Kickoff team general information

(a) How can we best return kickoffs versus the opponent's coverage team?
(b) Do they over-pursue and lose correct angles on the ball?
(c) Do they make special substitutions for onside kick attempts? Who?
(d) Any other vital information concerning opponent's kickoff coverage?

**The Kickoff Return Team**

   1. *Kickoff return alignment*

   (a)  Basic alignment (jersey numbers of return men and ends)
   (b)  Who is most dangerous return man? Where is he aligned?
        Who is second most dangerous? His alignment?
   (c)  Is alignment of personnel at either end position conducive
        to wide reverse?
   (d)  Does alignment lend itself to line driving ball at medium
        depth for bouncing kick? Where?
   (e)  Where should we kick onsides?

   2. *Kickoff return mechanics*

   (a)  Type return—Wedge? Wall? Reverse?
   (b)  Type blocking used
   (c)  Do backs ever cross for fake handoffs?
   (d)  Do linemen tip type of return? How?
   (e)  Do any of the linemen start toward blocking assignment
        before ball passes to them? Who?

   3. *Kickoff return general information*

   (a)  Which return man has worst hands?
   (b)  Do they insert a "hands" team in possible onsides kick
        situation?
   (c)  Any other information on kickoff return team?

## EXTRA POINT

   One extra point may be the difference in winning, losing
or tying several close games in a season. For this reason, this
part of the kicking game should be scouted closely. Figure 12-3
depicts an extra point and field goal kicking information sheet.

**Extra Point Kicking Team**

   1. Basic formation (jersey numbers of kicker, holder, ends
and blocking backs)
   2. Depth of holder?
   3. Type kicker—Conventional or soccer? Height?

4. Center snap—Accuracy and consistency

5. Holder's hands and quickness? Is he a quarterback or passer?

6. Time from snap to kick (stopwatch)

7. Where can we block it?

8. Have they faked the kick and gone for two points from this formation? If so, how?

## Extra Point Defense

1. Basic alignment

2. How do they try to block?

3. Who are specific players we need to concentrate on?

4. How can we fake and go for two?

## FIELD GOAL

### Field Goal Kicking Team

(Report the same basic information as in the extra point formation except the maximum distance and accuracy of the kicker.)

### Field Goal Defense

How do they play their secondary?

(The other information will be the same as in the extra point defense.)

## SCOUTING THE KICKING GAME—LIMITED STAFF

If any phase of scouting can get away from a one- or two-man Scouting Crew in a hurry, it is the kicking game. The rapid changes from offense and defense to the punting game, and an extra point followed closely by the kickoff, can leave a Scout scratching his head and shuffling papers if he is not well organized. Figure 12-4 shows an excellent one-page combined kicking game sheet that will make it much simpler for one or two Scouts to work the kicking game.

## WRAP-UP

A blocked punt, a punt returned for a touchdown, a blocked extra point or field goal, a successful extra point or field goal, a kickoff returned for a touchdown or to set up one, and the successful recovery of an onsides kick are all possible game-breakers. Through the proper scouting of the kicking game and a well-organized, thoroughly practiced kicking game plan, one or several of the above-mentioned occurrences may result in the winning of many games during the season.

## PUNTING GAME SHEET

| No. | Distance | Foot | Times | Best Hang Time | Avg. Hang Time | Other |
|-----|----------|------|-------|----------------|----------------|-------|
| 1. | | | | | | |
| 2. | | | | | | |
| 3. | | | | | | |

Punting Team:

First Players to Ball_____Blocks or near blocks_____.

Fake Punt?_____Snapper's ability_____.

Time from snap to foot contact with ball (avg.)_____;slowest_____;fastest_____.

Alignment and Numbers:

Punt Return:

Do they attempt to block?_____Best return man_____.

Describe return:

Alignment and Numbers:

Figure 12-1

KICKOFF GAME SHEET

| No. | Distance | Hang Time | Times | Foot | Soccer or Conventional |
|-----|----------|-----------|-------|------|------------------------|
| 1.  |          |           |       |      |                        |
| 2.  |          |           |       |      |                        |
| 3.  |          |           |       |      |                        |

### Diagram Kickoff Alignment and Numbers

Kick from middle or hash?_____Across or straight downfield?_____
Designated safety?_____First players to ball?_____
Cover in lanes?_____Other_____

### Diagram Kickoff Return

Best return man_____Do they wedge, wall, reverse, other?_____
Comments:

Alignment and numbers:

Figure 12-2

## EXTRA POINT AND FIELD GOAL SHEET

| Kickers No. | Distance | Height | Foot | Style | Accuracy | Other |
|---|---|---|---|---|---|---|
| 1. | | | | | | |
| 2. | | | | | | |
| 3. | | | | | | |

Attempt:

How can we block?

Do they ever fake the attempt? Explain.

Alignment and nos.

Defense and block attempt:

Players close to blocking kick_____

Alignment and nos.

Figure 12-3

COMBINED KICKING GAME SHEET

Kickoff Coverage                              Kickoff Return

35_____          _____ 40
40_____          _____ 50
                                             _____ 40
                                             _____ 30
                                             _____ 20
                                             _____ 10
                                             _____ G

Indicate men down exceptionally fast.

Punt Protection                                    Punt Return

PAT Protection                                     Punt Block

Figure 12-4

# 13

# HOW TO SCOUT THE GAME
## (Scouting Coach)

CHAPTERS 4, 5 and 6 have provided the Scouting Coach with the necessary ingredients to be effectively and thoroughly familiar with the team he is to scout, even before he sees them play. Through the assembling of information during the off-season, pre-season and early in-season, the Scout should have a detailed collection of vital material gathered with reference to the opponent designated to be scouted. A list of this information and its sources will include

1. Last year's film breakdown analysis;
2. Returning personnel evaluation reports (names, numbers, positions, abilities, strengths and weaknesses);
3. Spring training intra-squad game scout report (if applicable);
4. Pre-season scrimmage scout report (if applicable);
5. Pre-season magazine and newspaper publicity and predictions (these are good for many reasons, especially in getting the opponent's coach's views concerning his own players, etc.);
6. New personnel evaluation report (combine this with returning personnel report; pay particular attention to probable starter's jersey numbers);
7. In-season newspaper articles (game results, statistics, coachs' and players' comments, injuries, new personnel, changes, trick plays and anything else that might be helpful);
8. Discussions with scouts from other teams. Often, fellow scouts have seen your next opponent play several games. In

having done so, they may have picked up tip-offs, tendencies and other information that may be very helpful to your own report.

All this information should be studied by the Scout for at least a week prior to scouting the designated opponent. Using a tape recorder will be very helpful at this point, for the Scout can listen to tape recorded material in many instances when he cannot study printed information. Particular attention should be paid to learning the jersey numbers of the opponent's best athletes and worst athletes, the basic offensive and defensive sets, and the basic kicking game. Then, when the Scout works the game, he will be able to notice many other things because the basics will already be set in his mind.

## GATHERING THE MATERIALS

During the week before the designated opponent is to be scouted, the Scouts who will work the game should gather all the necessary materials together, early. Doing this early is important for several reasons.

1. Other Scouting Crews will be picking up their materials also. Any shortage of forms or other materials should be recognized and remedied early in the week.
2. With the pre-scouting material the Scout has built up already, early in the week he can further familiarize himself with the forms to be used and the prior knowledge he has of the designated opponent.
3. When scouting a team for the second or third time, the Scouting Coach can begin the compilation of his material early. This will allow him to assimilate the leftover forms, cards, etc., so he can tell exactly what materials he needs to scout the next game.
4. The earlier in the week the Scouting Coach gets his mind on his assigned job, the better he will do when game time comes.

Following is a tentative list of materials the Scouting Crew or Scouting Coach will take on a scouting trip. (These will, of course, vary in number and with thoroughness of information required, according to the number of coaches scouting the game.)

1. Scout Report forms (booklet)
   (a) Warm-up and general information sheet
   (b) Personnel sheets (starters and evaluation forms)
   (c) Basic offensive and defensive sets sheet
   (d) Variations—offensive sets and defensive alignments sheet
   (e) Offensive and defensive summary sheets
   (f) Kicking game sheets
   (g) Tip-offs and unusual action sheets
2. Recording forms (play by play on cards or individual sheets)
3. Plenty of pencils and at least two pens
4. Binoculars
5. Sound tape recorder
6. Stopwatches
7. Clipboard or notebook (keep paper work organized)
8. Extra paper for notes, diagrams, tip-offs, and other quick scribbles that can be so helpful later.
9. Hole punch (if punch card recording system is used)

Some Head Coaches like to keep close track of the scouting materials which are checked out each week by the Scouts. If tape recorders, stopwatches and binoculars are used, the Head Coach may want to issue these scouting materials by means of using check-out/check-in list system. Figure 13-1 shows an example of a scouting materials check-out/check-in form. Staff size and Scouting Crew size will determine whether such a check-out list is necessary.

## THE TRIP

All the coaches who are to scout an opponent should always travel to and from the game together. This will facilitate an information-transfer between the coaches as they are traveling. From the pre-scouting material they have been studying for the previous week, they can exchange ideas. Many helpful thoughts often come from such scouting travel discussions. If only one coach is going to scout for a limited size staff, he can listen to the material he has collected on the tape recorder as he travels to the game.

Following is a basic itinerary for a Scouting Crew traveling to scout a game:

1. Check all material to make sure you have all the necessary items.
2. Review pre-scouting material about opponent to be scouted for a last-minute refresher.
3. View a portion of film on the opponent. (Seeing them in action, even on film, will sharpen what the Scout already knows about them and will prepare the Scout's mind for the game ahead.)
4. Be sure to leave early enough to arrive at the game site at least an hour before the kickoff.
5. While traveling, discuss the opponents for information-transfer. (Many good thoughts come from such an exchange.)
6. Eat a pre-game meal in the city or town where the game is to be played. This is important for these reasons:
    (a) This will be a good time and place to buy a newspaper for an article about the team being scouted (for further information and for game plan display).
    (b) Pick an eating establishment (if possible) where cars or buses are decorated with the opponent's school slogans or school colors. (When inside, strike up conversations with various people from opponent's city or school. Many times, valuable information can be picked up simply through such gossip sessions. Particularly helpful information can be uncovered concerning fresh injuries, last-minute lineup changes, disciplinary actions, team morale, a star player's idiosyncrasies, etc.)
    (c) Planning to eat in the city or town where the game will be played allows the Scouting Crew ample time to deal with unexpected situations (flat tire, boilover, etc.)
7. Get to stadium at least one hour before kickoff!

## WORKING THE GAME

For the Scouting Coach or the Scouting Crew, this section is what scouting is actually all about. The importance of doing an excellent job of securing pertinent information concerning the opponents cannot be emphasized enough. The following pages contain a basic breakdown of the duties of the Scouting Crew before, during, and after a game.

The remainder of this chapter provides the correct order and basic technique for general information-gathering methods to be used by the Scouting Coach or Scouting Crew. Preceding chapters have detailed the specific techniques of gathering the exact information about each intricate phase of the game. Therefore, the order of events is what is important here, with only the basic general information-gathering techniques listed for better clarity.

## Pre-Game Preparation

As soon as the Scouting Crew enters the stadium, there are several items which should be taken care of immediately. These include:

1. Buying at least five game programs;
2. Making film exchange with opponents being scouted (if applicable);
3. Being sure to get a place in the press box early to avoid scrambling for a seat while the team is warming up;
4. If scouting in a Crew, having one or two of the Scouting Coaches save places in the press box while the others work the field to pick up:
   a. Snap count (get variances in count and anything unusual)
   b. Actual size estimates of players (whether they are larger or smaller than listed in program)
   c. Specific habits of quarterbacks, receivers, etc. that can be used as tip-offs
   d. Line splits and defensive shades in pre-game work (if either not available at this time, get them just before or after the half)
   e. Team morale and enthusiasm
   If a coach is scouting alone, he can get a scout from another school to save him a place while picking up the above-mentioned information on the field. (He should also check-in with the person in charge of the press box to make sure his

place is reserved.) The Scout should take the scouting booklet with him so he can gather warm-up information.

5. Talk to other scouts, fans, school personnel, and any other knowledgeable people, to gain any other final bits of information before the actual pre-game warm-up and your work begins.

## Use the Shorthand System

As was elaborated on earlier, the Scouting Crew should use the shorthand system in writing information about the opponents. The particular type of system is not important; whatever the staff decides upon is fine. The important thing is that a well-organized shorthand system will allow a good Scouting Crew to record from 33 to 50 percent more valuable information about the opponents than they would be able to get using the longhand method.

## The Warm-Up Period

When the team being scouted takes the field, the Scouting Crew should gather the following information during the warm-up period and record it in the appropriate places in the scouting booklet. (Turn on the sound tape recorder for reinforcement information.) Remember that from this point on, only the general order of items to be covered are listed in this chapter. They have been covered in detail in preceding chapters.

1. Get general weather and field conditions
2. Passers—jersey numbers and specifics on ability
3. Receivers—jersey numbers and specifics on ability
4. Punters and Snappers—jersey numbers and specifics on ability
5. Extra Point and Field Goal—jersey numbers and specifics on ability
6. Kickoff—jersey numbers and specifics on ability
7. Punt and Kick Receivers—jersey numbers and specifics on ability
8. Team Leaders—jersey numbers and role
9. Injuries—jersey numbers and type of apparent injuries
10. Anything special or unusual

## Compare Your Personnel with Theirs While Scouting

Earlier, in Chapter 8, "How to Train Coaches Who Scout," the importance of knowing your own personnel while scouting was discussed. To do an equitable job of scouting, the Scout must compare the personnel on the opponent's team with his own team's personnel as the game progresses. If this is not done, no Scout can give a creditable scout report. For example, the designated opponent's defensive left tackle may be destroying the opposing team's tackle during the game being scouted. If the Scout does not realize that his own team's right offensive tackle is an excellent blocker, and can handle their tackle, he will erroneously tell the staff they cannot run in this area against the designated opponents. Therefore, know the personnel abilities of your team and make use of this knowledge while scouting.

## First Half

The Scouting Crew's working procedure will depend on the number of Scouts available. If there are at least three Scouts working the game, they may operate in this manner:

1. Scout number one—writes down all offensive information and calls out all defensive information
2. Scout number two—writes down all defensive information and calls out all offensive information
3. Scout number three and/or number four—work personnel, tip-offs, kicking game, other intricacies, and back up Scouts one and two when help is needed

If there are two Scouts, follow the procedure of Scouts one and two above, with both working the kicking game. Personnel, tip-offs, etc., must be worked in, especially in the second half.

If scouting alone, the Scout must get as much of the pertinent information as possible. Here, the scouting forms must be arranged for rapid use. Sheets with room for a series of downs, rather than individual play cards, etc., should be used.

Regardless of the number of Scouts working, the major item to keep in mind is that you must find the areas that can be exploited, in every phase of the game, and be sure to get this information recorded.

At the flip of the coin, prepare the kickoff or receiving sheet according to the results of the flip. Record the appropriate kickoff personnel, coverage, and return information before and after the kickoff. Let us presume the designated opponents who are being scouted are on offense first. The offensive information in the following list should be recorded on each play if possible. (Remember, if the Scout is working alone, the most important thing is to get play action and down and distance unless the film of that same game is available; if this is so, then he can gather other specific information.)

1. Down and distance
2. Spot on field (yard line)
3. Hash placement
4. Formation
5. Play action (backs and linemen)
6. Ball carrier, passer and/or receiver
7. Yardage gained or lost
8. Any type motion or shift
9. Anything unusual of significance
10. Substitutions
11. Penalty (type and against whom)
12. Punting game
13. Formulate an answer in your mind, as the game progresses, to the question, "What Must We Stop?"

Defensively, get the following facts:

1. Basic front;
2. Number and placement of linebackers;
3. Secondary alignment and basic coverage (zone, man). Once these have been established, proceed to break down the defense as the game moves on. Most teams today use multiple sets on defense. However, it will not take long to discern the designated opponent's defensive strategy, especially if it is similar to that which the Scout has been studying since the off-season.

The Scouting Crew should continue to gain and record further findings about the opponent's defense such as:

1. Down and distance tendencies
2. Field and boundary tendencies
3. Tendencies formulated by their opponent's offensive formations
4. Short yardage, long yardage and prevent situation tendencies
5. Field zone tendencies
6. Personnel (best, worst, etc.)
7. Punt receiving game
8. Find out the opponent's vulnerable areas so you can answer the question, "Where Can We Move It?" for the Offensive Coordinator. Be sure to jot down notes when anything takes place that is not accounted for on the scouting forms. Also, if the on-field action is moving too rapidly to write such notes and keep up with the play-by-play information, use the tape recorder to secure these facts.

## Half Time

At the half, the Scouting Crew should go back through all the information gathered since their arrival at the stadium. This material should be reorganized and any important ideas that were jotted down should be assimilated into the report in the proper places. Then, the forms, cards, and/or other various kinds of materials that the Scouts are using should be readied for the second half of play. Discussion between the Scouting Crew should yield further information and ideas. Then, the Scouts should talk with other scouts and possibly add new information. Be sure to record all information not on paper with the tape player.

## Second Half

The scouting process during the second half will be much the same as it was in the first half. Familiarity with the opponent's maneuvers, however, should allow the Scouts to pay more attention to the intricacies of offensive and defensive schemes. The Scouts can write down the vital information as they do during the first half and also be able to pick up new information as to

1. Personnel (strengths and weaknesses);
2. Individual standouts (what they do best);

3. Boundary and field tendencies of the offense;
4. Tip-offs;
5. Unusual habits, sets or maneuvers;
6. Exact alignments or movements by specific personnel (offensive line splits, defensive front sets, secondary rotation, etc.).

## Post-Game Analysis

One of the most important phases of scouting a game is the post-game analysis. This quick wrap-up of information, ideas and other factors should take place immediately after the game is concluded. This analysis is simply a review of the events of the game, adding any information necessary by use of notes or the tape recorder and putting the report in order for the next phase, which is compilation of information. When these processes are completed, the Scouting Crew should synthesize the analysis by seriously discussing the strengths and weaknesses of the upcoming opponents. This session should be aimed at answering the question, "How Can We Win?"

As the coaches leave the stadium, they should pick up several game programs which have been left by fans. The extra programs can be used for cutting out pictures for personnel rosters to be posted in the field house.

## FILM CONFIRMATION

In areas where film trades are practiced, the Scouting Crew, upon arrival back at its own field house, can view the traded film to confirm play action from their scout report. Film is especially helpful in verifying line blocking, defensive alignments, and all receivers in pass routes. When the Scouting Crew completes the film confirmation, they should go home for a few hours of sleep before compiling all the information for transfer to the staff the next morning.

## THE ONE-MAN SCOUTING SYSTEM

When only one man is sent to scout an upcoming opponent, he has to approach the task much differently than does the Scouting Crew of three or four coaches. The lone Scout has to accumulate all the aforementioned information possible, by himself. For this reason, the forms, methods and techniques used by the Scout will of necessity be simpler in format with less total information required. A very creditable job of scouting can be accomplished by one coach if he is very organized and knows what information he wants to collect.

He simply cannot be as thorough as a complete Scouting Crew, so he must forego getting information not necessary, and be sure to record (on paper and/or on tape) the vital information needed. This too will vary, for some limited number staffs have access to film; some do not. If film is available, more attention can be paid to strengths, weaknesses, tip-offs and other specifics. If film is not available, the Scout must stay strongly with the play-by-play report forms. Preceding chapters include forms, methods and information collection techniques for the one-man scouting system as well as those for the fully manned scouting systems.

## WRAP-UP

Regardless of the size of a Scouting Crew, the one most important ingredient for each coach to realize is to be dedicated to the cause of scouting. If a coach works to be a competent scout, he can help the varsity win against the opponents.

However, if a Scouting Crew puts anything ahead of excellence in its scouting endeavor, it will hurt its team. For instance, some coaches who scout are so interested in eating at a particular restaurant that they do not do any preparation work (film viewing, etc.) before leaving home. Many times, coaches who fit this category get to the stadium late and leave before the game is over. Coaches who fit this mold usually use the half time for wandering around or stuffing down food.

The above statements may seem rather harsh, but coaches who scout in this manner will not formulate a reliable scout report. In fact, these types of Scouting Crews often help cause a poor game plan with incomplete or incorrect information.

Be a dedicated scout and you will soon become a more successful coach. The good Scout learns a great deal about

football and also becomes very organized. These are both keys
to becoming a successful, winning Coach.

Remember, when scouting, prepare thoroughly, record
everything immediately; never guess, tell it like it is and you
will always be a reliable Scout! Also remember that the entire
process of scouting a team (off-season, pre-season, in-season
and the actual scouting of the game) is all done to answer the
following questions correctly:

1. Where Can We Move It?
2. What Must We Stop?
3. How Can We Win?

**MASTER SCOUTING MATERIALS CHECK OUT - IN CHART**

| Materials | Crew #1 | | Crew #2 | | Crew #3 | | |
|---|---|---|---|---|---|---|---|
| | Out | In | Out | In | Out | In | |
| Scouting Booklet | | | | | | | |
| Cards and Sheets | | | | | | | |
| Clipboard Notebook #1 | | | X | X | X | X | |
| Clipboard Notebook #2 | X | X | | | X | X | |
| Clipboard Notebook #3 | X | X | X | X | | | |
| Binoculars #1 | | | X | X | X | X | |
| Binoculars #2 | X | X | | | X | X | |
| Binoculars #3 | X | X | X | X | | | |
| Sound Recorder #1 | | | X | X | X | X | |
| Sound Recorder #2 | X | X | | | X | X | |
| Sound Recorder #3 | X | X | X | X | | | |
| Stop Watch #1 | | | X | X | X | X | |
| Stop Watch #2 | X | X | | | X | X | |
| Stop Watch #3 | X | X | X | X | | | |
| Hole Punch #1 | | | X | X | X | X | |
| Hole Punch #2 | X | X | | | X | X | |
| Hole Punch #3 | X | X | X | X | | | |

Figure 13-1

# 14

# HOW TO COMPILE THE INFORMATION
## (Staff and Scouts)

### THE COMPILING PROCESS

THE compiling process will, of course, differ a great deal from staff to staff according to the type of scouting system used. For example, compiling a computerized system is relatively simple because the printouts of the various tendencies can be read and noted without actually compiling the information manually. A standard system on the other hand, requires the scout to do the assimilation and compilation of information himself to render the desired information about the opponent's tendencies.

Regardless of the system used, the important thing to remember about the compiling process is that it must yield information about the opponent's tendencies, which will be all-important in the game-planning process. For this reason, the Scouts working the compiling process should be sure that they secure the specific information needed by the Varsity Staff.

Since the compiling process will vary a great deal from staff to staff, the basic categories of offense, defense and kicking game tendencies will be covered here, with the forms shown, which were selected so that they may be used in any type of scouting system. Also, the Scouts should be sure to use the scouting booklet information in the compiling process.

## Programming the Computer for Compilation

There are several methods by which computerized scouting information may be programmed for compilation. One popular method is to code all information taken so that it will be compatible with the terminal. Another method is for one of the staff members to take the scouting information to the terminal and either program the computer himself or let an operator do so.

Still another method makes use of the team's own (or the school system's) computer. This method is operated entirely within the staff or within the team's own school system. (Those staffs not now using the computer scouting method should check into these possibilities. Many school systems now have computers. Also, small, inexpensive computer terminals can be purchased through the football budget.) Still other teams use a professional scouting service. With this method, much of the assimilation and programming duties are the responsibilities of the service, while other services are responsible for the entire package.

The computer compilation method yields several types of results. Many systems produce some type of printout which coaches can work from in game planning. Another less expensive method entails having members of the staff copy the information from the terminal screen. Cost considerations will determine the method used, in most cases.

## COMPILING OFFENSIVE TENDENCIES

### Personnel Summary

In compiling the offense, the Scouts should finalize all the information on the opponent's offensive personnel, including all the games scouted. Figure 14-1 shows a personnel summary form on which the opponent's starting personnel, substitutions, characteristics and abilities can be recorded.

### Formation Tendencies

In compiling formation tendencies, some of the information which should be noted includes:

1. All formations;
2. Times each used;
3. Percentage each formation used;
4. Favorite plays from each formation:
   (a) Run
   (b) Pass
5. Any personnel tendencies revealed by formations.

This kind of information will help determine what the opponents may do in certain formations. Figures 14-2, 14-3 and 14-4 illustrate forms that can be used to develop formations used and tendencies.

## Down and Distance Tendencies

Probably one of the most important offensive tendencies is what the opponents do by down and distance. This type of tendency can be done simply by compiling the down and distance and the play run in each situation. Figures 14-5 and 14-6 depict forms on which this information can be compiled. Figure 14-7 shows a form on which not only down and distance but also hash, formation, type of play and other information can be compiled. This form offers a much more thorough look at what the opponents do by down and distance. In Figure 14-7, only first down situations are used. Other forms of the same type are used for the various down and distance situations in this system of compiling.

## Hash Mark and Field Position Tendencies

In working hash mark tendencies, the Scouts should compile the information so as to provide the Varsity Staff with knowledge of any tendencies set by the opponents with respect to hash mark location. Figure 14-8 illustrates a form which will yield important information as to where and how the opponents attack from the various hash mark locations. Figure 14-9 shows a form which can be used to note both hash mark and field position tendencies.

## Combined Tendencies

Some systems like to combine several tendencies on one form. Figure 14-10 depicts a hash mark and formation tendency chart which also can be used to determine point of attack by hash and formation, percentage each formation is run on each hash, passes thrown from each hash, and the percentage of time each area was attacked from each hash position. Figure 14-11 illustrates an offensive color chart which provides the formation (through color-coding the backs and holes attacked), best plays from the formation, which area each back attacked, yardage gained on each effort, and the average yards gained in the formation. (This is accomplished by coloring each back differently with marking pens and then, with the color which corresponds to each back, recording the yardage gained in the various areas he attacked.) This information is compiled and recorded for each formation used, and provides a good overall picture of the opponent's offense.

### Accumulated Offensive Analysis

Figure 14-12 shows an excellent form for compiling the opponent's total offensive production for the Varsity Staff's analysis. This is an excellent way to wrap up the compilation of the opposing team's various offensive tendencies. The accumulated offensive analysis can provide information which may not always appear on the tendency charts and helps reveal the entire offensive picture of the opponents.

## COMPILING DEFENSIVE TENDENCIES

### Personnel Summary

A defensive personnel summary such as the one shown in Figure 14-13 should be prepared by the Scouts as part of the defensive compilation. All available information about the opponent's defensive personnel should be included in this summary.

### Defensive Alignment Tendencies

Figure 14-14 illustrates a form which can be used to compile the defensive alignment tendencies of the opponents. In compiling the defensive alignment tendencies, the Scouts should include all alignments, variations, adjustments and

stunts. The percentage each is used can also be recorded for
tendency purposes.

### Defensive Basic Reaction Tendencies

From the scouting information, because of the nature of
defense, it will be helpful to describe the basic defensive
reactions of the opponents. Figures 14-15 and 14-16 provide
examples of forms that can be used to outline the basic
reactions of the opponent's defensive front and secondary,
respectively. (In some cases, such as a limited Scouting Crew
or one Scout working alone, this form can be very helpful in
getting important defensive information compiled on the
opponents.)

### Secondary Analysis

An increasingly important factor in compiling defensive
material is the analysis of secondary coverages. Figure 14-17
depicts a form which covers secondary alignments, coverages,
whether man-to-man or zone was used, and the percentage
used. This chart also covers the all-important aspects of goal
line coverages and prevent coverages.

### Special Defensive Alignments

The defenses used by the opponents in special situations
deserve attention during the defensive compilation process.
Short yardage, goal line and prevent alignments should be
carefully charted, and specific strengths and weaknesses
noted. Figure 14-18 shows a form which can be used for this
purpose.

### Down and Distance Tendencies

After all the alignment analysis is done, a down and
distance chart should be compiled to develop tendencies on
the opponents in this important area. By this time, all the
defensive alignments, adjustments, variations and stunts
should be listed and can be numbered and therefore charted
easily as to down and distance. Figure 14-19 illustrates a
simple down and distance compiling form.

## Field Position and Hash Mark Tendencies

Figure 14-20 shows a chart on which the opponent's defensive alignments can be tendencied by where they are used on the field. This information can be very important in game planning. Another important tendency which should be compiled at this time is the frequency of use of the various defensive alignments on the hash mark locations. This compilation will often reveal important information as to how the opponents attempt to defend the wide side of the field and the boundary. Figure 14-21 depicts a chart which can be used to tendency the opponent's hash mark location defensive alignments.

## Accumulated Defensive Analysis

It would be wise, after the opponent's defense has been compiled and tendencied, to record an accumulated defensive analysis chart such as the one shown in Figure 14-22. This chart will sum up the opponent's defensive successes and failures and will be helpful in picturing their overall defensive capability. Some of this information may have to be taken from newspaper accounts of the game that was scouted because the Scouts are not likely to have the time to gather all the statistics necessary for the defensive analysis chart.

## COMPILING THE KICKING GAME

Since the kicking game is covered in the pre-game information and again during the game as to personnel and performance, the compilation of the kicking game should be rather simple. The following list shows some categories which should be compiled.

1. Average depth of kickoff            _____
2. Average kickoff return point         _____
3. Onsides attempts                     _____
4. Average punt distance                _____
5. Average punt return distance         _____
6. Fakes off punt (if so, explain)      _____
7. Opponent's punts blocked             _____

8. Punts blocked by opponents          _____
9. Field goals (distance)  _____ _____ _____ _____

                                        _____
10. Fakes off field goal formation (explain)     _____
11. Fakes off extra point formation (explain)    _____

## WRAP-UP

After the major portions of the compilation process mentioned in this chapter are done, there are other duties which should be completed by the Scouts. Some of these may include:

1. Making personnel poster
2. Making favorite formations and alignment posters
3. Making best plays and pass patterns poster
4. Completing any other compilation work desired by the Varsity Staff

Also, another phase of the compiling process is the confirming of the scout report by the use of film (if available). This practice will make the Scouts' work easier, especially in cases such as complicated defensive stunts or slants, or an offensive play on which there was one or more pulling lineman. This viewing of the game film also makes the Scouts' work valid.

Once all the compilation is finished, the Scouts are then ready to transfer the information to the Varsity Staff.

**OFFENSIVE PERSONNEL SUMMARY SHEET**

Opponents Scouted_____

| Position | Name | No. | Wt. | Remarks |
|---|---|---|---|---|
| Left or Split End | 1.<br>2. | | | |
| Right or Tight End | 1.<br>2. | | | |
| Left Tackle | 1.<br>2. | | | |
| Left Guard | 1.<br>2. | | | |
| Center | 1.<br>2. | | | |
| Right Guard | 1.<br>2. | | | |
| Right Tackle | 1.<br>2. | | | |
| Quarterback | 1.<br>2. | | | |
| Running Back | 1.<br>2. | | | |
| Fullback | 1.<br>2. | | | |
| Flanker, Slot or 4th Back | 1.<br>2. | | | |

Figure 14-1

## FORMATIONS CHART

Opponent_____

(Number Same As On Play-By-Play Cards)


1._____  % Used___    2._____  % Used___




3._____  % Used___    4._____  % Used___




5._____  % Used___    6._____  % Used___




7._____  % Used___    8._____  % Used___




9._____  % Used___    10._____  % Used___


Figure 14-2

**FORMATION TENDENCY CHART**
Opponent Scouted_____

**Formations Used**

Formation_____
No. Times_____
% Used_____

Formation_____
No. Times_____
% Used_____

Formation_____
No. Times_____
% Used_____

Formation_____
No. Times_____
% Used_____

Formation_____
No. Times_____
% Used_____

Formation_____
No. Times_____
% Used_____

Figure 14-3

## FORMATION TENDENCY CHART

Opponents Scouted_____

Formation_____

| Running Plays | Times Used |
|---|---|
|  |  |
|  |  |
|  |  |
|  |  |
|  |  |
|  |  |
|  |  |

Defense To Use

1.

2.

3.

4.

5.

### Passing Plays

| Series | Patterns | Times Used |
|---|---|---|
|  |  |  |
|  |  |  |
|  |  |  |
|  |  |  |
|  |  |  |

Defense To Use

1.

2.

3.

4.

5.

Favorite Back_____His Best Play_____

Favorite Receiver_____His Best Pattern_____

Figure 14-4

DOWN AND DISTANCE TENDENCY CHART

Opponent Scouted_____

| 1st & 10 | | 1st & 10 + | | 1st & 5 | | Remarks |
|---|---|---|---|---|---|---|
| Play Times | Play Times | Play Times | Play Times | Play Times | Play Times | |
| ___ ___ | ___ ___ | ___ ___ | ___ ___ | ___ ___ | ___ ___ | |
| ___ ___ | ___ ___ | ___ ___ | ___ ___ | ___ ___ | ___ ___ | |
| ___ ___ | ___ ___ | ___ ___ | ___ ___ | ___ ___ | ___ ___ | |
| ___ ___ | ___ ___ | ___ ___ | ___ ___ | ___ ___ | ___ ___ | |
| ___ ___ | ___ ___ | ___ ___ | ___ ___ | ___ ___ | ___ ___ | |
| Number of Passes ___ | | Number of Passes ___ | | Number of Passes ___ | | |

| 2nd & 7-10 | | 2nd & 4-6 | | 2nd & 1-3 | | 2nd & 10 + | |
|---|---|---|---|---|---|---|---|
| Play Times | Play Times | Play Times | Play Times | Play Times | Play Times | Play Times | Play Times |
| ___ ___ | ___ ___ | ___ ___ | ___ ___ | ___ ___ | ___ ___ | ___ ___ | ___ ___ |
| ___ ___ | ___ ___ | ___ ___ | ___ ___ | ___ ___ | ___ ___ | ___ ___ | ___ ___ |
| ___ ___ | ___ ___ | ___ ___ | ___ ___ | ___ ___ | ___ ___ | ___ ___ | ___ ___ |
| ___ ___ | ___ ___ | ___ ___ | ___ ___ | ___ ___ | ___ ___ | ___ ___ | ___ ___ |
| Number of Passes ___ | | Number of Passes ___ | | Number of Passes ___ | | Number of Passes ___ | |

| 3rd & 7-10 | | 3rd & 4-6 | | 3rd & 1-3 | | 3rd & 10 + | |
|---|---|---|---|---|---|---|---|
| Play Times | Play Times | Play Times | Play Times | Play Times | Play Times | Play Times | Play Times |
| ___ ___ | ___ ___ | ___ ___ | ___ ___ | ___ ___ | ___ ___ | ___ ___ | ___ ___ |
| ___ ___ | ___ ___ | ___ ___ | ___ ___ | ___ ___ | ___ ___ | ___ ___ | ___ ___ |
| ___ ___ | ___ ___ | ___ ___ | ___ ___ | ___ ___ | ___ ___ | ___ ___ | ___ ___ |
| ___ ___ | ___ ___ | ___ ___ | ___ ___ | ___ ___ | ___ ___ | ___ ___ | ___ ___ |
| Number of Passes ___ | | Number of Passes ___ | | Number of Passes ___ | | Number of Passes ___ | |

| 4th & 7-10 | | 4th & 4-6 | | 4th & 1-3 | | 4th & 10 + | |
|---|---|---|---|---|---|---|---|
| Play Times | Play Times | Play Times | Play Times | Play Times | Play Times | Play Times | Play Times |
| ___ ___ | ___ ___ | ___ ___ | ___ ___ | ___ ___ | ___ ___ | ___ ___ | ___ ___ |
| ___ ___ | ___ ___ | ___ ___ | ___ ___ | ___ ___ | ___ ___ | ___ ___ | ___ ___ |
| ___ ___ | ___ ___ | ___ ___ | ___ ___ | ___ ___ | ___ ___ | ___ ___ | ___ ___ |
| ___ ___ | ___ ___ | ___ ___ | ___ ___ | ___ ___ | ___ ___ | ___ ___ | ___ ___ |
| Number of Passes ___ | | Number of Passes ___ | | Number of Passes ___ | | Number of Passes ___ | |

Figure 14-5

DOWN AND DISTANCE TENDENCY CHART

Opponent Scouted_____

Plays and Times Run

| Down & Distance | Play Times | Play Times | Play Times | Play Times | Play Times | Play Times | Play Times | Play Times |
|---|---|---|---|---|---|---|---|---|
| 1st & 10 + | | | | | | | | |
| 1st & 10 | | | | | | | | |
| 1st & 5 | | | | | | | | |
| 2nd & 10 + | | | | | | | | |
| 2nd & 7-10 | | | | | | | | |
| 2nd & 4-6 | | | | | | | | |
| 2nd & 1-3 | | | | | | | | |
| 3rd & 10 + | | | | | | | | |
| 3rd & 7-10 | | | | | | | | |
| 3rd & 4-6 | | | | | | | | |
| 3rd & 1-3 | | | | | | | | |
| 4th & 10 + | | | | | | | | |
| 4th & 7-10 | | | | | | | | |
| 4th & 4-6 | | | | | | | | |
| 4th & 1-3 | | | | | | | | |
| Goal Line  3-5 Yd.Ln. | | | | | | | | |
| Goal Line  1-2 Yd.Ln. | | | | | | | | |

Figure 14-6

## DOWN AND DISTANCE TENDENCY CHART

### 1st and 10

| Number | Hash | Formation | Run Pass | Yardage | Play | Ball Carrier | Remarks |
|--------|------|-----------|----------|---------|------|--------------|---------|
| 1 | | | | | | | |
| 2 | | | | | | | |
| 3 | | | | | | | |
| 4 | | | | | | | |
| 5 | | | | | | | |
| 6 | | | | | | | |
| 7 | | | | | | | |
| 8 | | | | | | | |
| 9 | | | | | | | |
| 10 | | | | | | | |
| 11 | | | | | | | |
| 12 | | | | | | | |
| 13 | | | | | | | |
| 14 | | | | | | | |
| 15 | | | | | | | |

### 1st and 5

| Number | Hash | Formation | Run Pass | Yardage | Play | Ball Carrier | Remarks |
|--------|------|-----------|----------|---------|------|--------------|---------|
| 1 | | | | | | | |
| 2 | | | | | | | |
| 3 | | | | | | | |
| 4 | | | | | | | |
| 5 | | | | | | | |
| 6 | | | | | | | |
| 7 | | | | | | | |

Figure 14-7

## HASH MARK TENDENCY CHART

Opponent Scouted _____

### Running Game

**Left Hash**

| 8 | 6 | 4 | 2 | 0 | 1 | 3 | 5 | 7 | 9 |
|---|---|---|---|---|---|---|---|---|---|
|   |   |   |   |   |   |   |   |   |   |
|   |   |   |   |   |   |   |   |   |   |

Attack To Boundary _____ %
Attack To Field _____ %
Formation Used Most _____

### Middle

Attack To Defensive Left _____ %
Attack To Defensive Right _____ %
Formation Used Most _____

**Right Hash**

| 9 | 7 | 5 | 3 | 1 | 0 | 2 | 4 | 6 | 8 |
|---|---|---|---|---|---|---|---|---|---|
|   |   |   |   |   |   |   |   |   |   |
|   |   |   |   |   |   |   |   |   |   |

Attack To Boundary _____ %
Attack To Field _____ %
Formation Used Most _____

### Passing Game

**Left Hash**

| L. Flat | L. Hook | R. Hook | R. Flat |
|---------|---------|---------|---------|
| Outside 1/3 | Middle 1/3 | | Outside 1/3 |

Favorite Rec. _____ Pos. _____
Favorite Patterns 1. _____
2. _____
3. _____

**Middle**

| L. Flat | L. Hook | R. Hook | R. Flat |
|---------|---------|---------|---------|
| Outside 1/3 | Middle 1/3 | | Outside 1/3 |

Favorite Rec. _____ Pos. _____
Favorite Patterns 1. _____
2. _____
3. _____

**Right Hash**

| L. Flat | L. Hook | R. Hook | R. Flat |
|---------|---------|---------|---------|
| Outside 1/3 | Middle 1/3 | | Outside 1/3 |

Favorite Rec. _____ Pos. _____
Favorite Patterns 1. _____
2. _____
3. _____

Figure 14-8

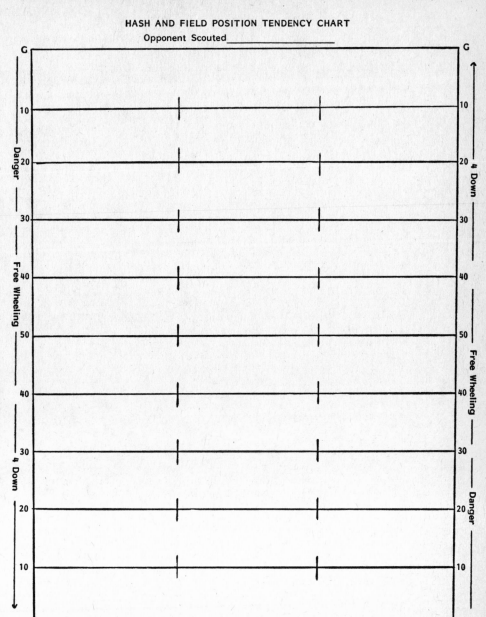

Figure 14-9

**HASH AND FORMATION TENDENCY CHART**

Opponent Scouted_____

Formation No.____Times Run____

Left Hash

Hole Attacked

% Attacked

Number of Passes Thrown_____

Middle

Formation No.____Times Run____

Hole Attacked

% Attacked

Number of Passes Thrown_____

Formation No.____Times Run____

Right Hash

Hole Attacked

% Attacked

Number of Passes Thrown_____

Figure 14-10

OFFENSIVE TENDENCY COLOR CHART

**Opponent Scouted**_____

**Formation**_____

**Best plays from this formation**_____ _____ _____

**Avg. yards per play**_____

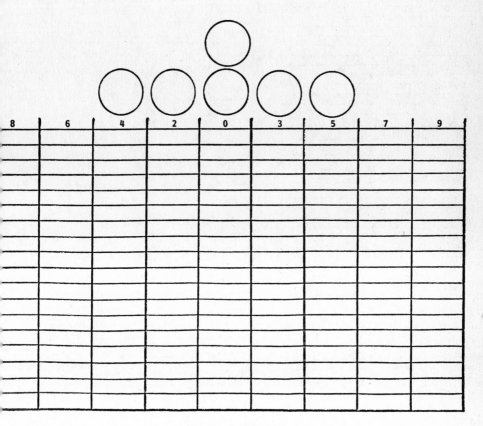

Figure 14-11

ACCUMULATIVE OFFENSIVE ANALYSIS CHART

Opponents _____

| RUSHING GAME | | |
|---|---|---|
| Ball Carrier | Fum. | Yds. |
| | | |
| | | |
| | | |
| | | |
| | | |
| | | |
| | | |
| | | |
| | | |
| | | |
| | | |
| | | |
| | | |
| | | |
| | | |
| | | |
| | | |
| | | |
| | | |

**PASSING GAME**

| Passer | Att. | Comp. | Yds. | Inter. | Drops | Traps |
|---|---|---|---|---|---|---|
| | | | | | | |
| | | | | | | |

**SCORING**

| Player | T.D. | X. Point | F.G. | Safety |
|---|---|---|---|---|
| | | | | |

**PUNTS**

| Player | Distance |
|---|---|
| | |

**PENALTIES**

| Player | Type Pen. | Yardage |
|---|---|---|
| | | |

| PASSING GAME | | |
|---|---|---|
| Receiver | Fum. | Yds. |
| | | |
| | | |
| | | |
| | | |
| | | |
| | | |
| | | |
| | | |
| | | |
| | | |
| | | |
| | | |
| | | |

**KICK-OFF RETURNS          PUNT RETURNS**

| Player | Yardage | Player | Yardage |
|---|---|---|---|
| | | | |

**BALL CONTROL**

| Drive Began On: | Yd. Line | No. Plays in Drive |
|---|---|---|
| | | |

1st Downs:

Figure 14-12

DEFENSIVE PERSONNEL SUMMARY SHEET

Opponent Scouted_____

| Position | Name | No. | Wt. | Remarks |
|---|---|---|---|---|
| Left or Strong End | 1.<br>2. | | | |
| Right or Weak End | 1.<br>2. | | | |
| Left Tackle | 1.<br>2. | | | |
| Right Tackle | 1.<br>2. | | | |
| MLB or Nose | 1.<br>2. | | | |
| Left or Strong Linebacker | 1.<br>2. | | | |
| Right or Weak Linebacker | 1.<br>2. | | | |
| Left or Strong Corner | 1.<br>2. | | | |
| Strong Safety | 1.<br>2. | | | |
| Free Safety | 1.<br>2. | | | |
| Right or Weak Corner | 1.<br>2. | | | |

Figure 14-13

### PERCENTAGE USED DEFENSIVE ALIGNMENTS FORM

Opponent Scouted_____

Diagram all defensive alignments, variations and stunts.
List percentage each used.

1._____% Used                 5._____% Used

2._____% Used                 6._____% Used

3._____% Used                 7._____% Used

4._____% Used                 8._____% Used

Figure 14-14

DEFENSIVE FRONT BASIC REACTION FORM

Opponent Scouted_____

**1. Interior Line**
How far off ball?                    Go on snap or movement?
Anticipate count?                    Read or attack?
Charge high or low?                  Other observations (flip-flop,etc.)

**2. Defensive Ends**
Technique on:     Dropback pass

Flow away

Flow toward

Pinch or box?
Skate on option?
Option responsibility?
Close quickly when tight end blocks down?
Can he be hook blocked?
Pass responsibility?
Alignment when tight end flexes?
Alignment vs. tight wing?
Do they flip-flop?

**3. Linebackers**
Blitz?
Tipoff?
Depth of alignment: Normal_____Passing situation_____

Short yardage_____Special_____

Drop quickly on pass?
Middle backer drop to strong or weak side on dropback?

Other comments on defensive front:


Diagram basic front alignment and numbers:


Figure 14-15

## DEFENSIVE SECONDARY BASIC REACTION FORM

Opponent Scouted_____

| CORNERBACKS | STRONG | WEAK |
|---|---|---|
| Watch QB or receiver | | |
| Come quickly on flow | | |
| Bump and run | | |
| Responsibility on option | | |
| Do they flip-flop? | | |

STRONG SAFETY OR MONSTER

   Invert or roll?

   Back turned to flanker?

   Support quickly

   Man to man

   Responsibility on option

   Deep middle on flow away?

   Responsible for veer pass?

   Other observations:


Diagram basic alignment and numbers:


Figure 14-16

## SECONDARY ANALYSIS CHART

Opponent Scouted_____

Diagram Secondary Coverage Alignments; List Type Coverage and Percent Used

1._____% Used

Man_____Zone_____

4._____% Used

Man_____Zone_____

2._____% Used

Man_____Zone_____

5._____% Used

Man_____Zone_____

3._____% Used

Man_____Zone_____

6._____% Used

Man_____Zone_____

**Goal Line Coverage**

Man_____Zone_____

**Prevent Coverage**

Man_____Zone_____

Figure 14-17

**SPECIAL DEFENSIVE ALIGNMENTS CHART**
Opponents Scouted_____

Diagram special alignments and indicate charges and coverage areas

Short Yardage Alignment                    Short Yardage Variation

Goal Line Alignment                        Goal Line Variation

Prevent Alignment                          Prevent Variation

Figure 14-18

### DOWN AND DISTANCE DEFENSIVE ALIGNMENTS FORM

Opponent Scouted_____

List defensive alignments used by down and distance

| 1 & 10 | 2 & 5-10 | 2 & 1-4 | 3 & 4-10 | 3 & 1-3 | 4 & 1-3 | 1 & 5 | 1 & 10+ | Unusual |
|---|---|---|---|---|---|---|---|---|
| | | | | | | | | |
| | | | | | | | | |
| | | | | | | | | |
| | | | | | | | | |
| | | | | | | | | |
| | | | | | | | | |
| | | | | | | | | |
| | | | | | | | | |
| | | | | | | | | |
| | | | | | | | | |
| | | | | | | | | |
| | | | | | | | | |
| | | | | | | | | |
| | | | | | | | | |
| | | | | | | | | |
| | | | | | | | | |
| | | | | | | | | |
| | | | | | | | | |
| | | | | | | | | |
| | | | | | | | | |
| | | | | | | | | |
| | | | | | | | | |
| | | | | | | | | |
| | | | | | | | | |
| | | | | | | | | |
| | | | | | | | | |
| | | | | | | | | |
| | | | | | | | | |

Figure 14-19

FIELD  POSITION  DEFENSIVE  ALIGNMENT  CHART

Opponent  Scouted_____

List  Alignments  Used  And  Number  Times  Used  In  Each  Field  Zone

**0-30**

Alignment_____        Times Used_____

_____                _____

_____                _____

_____                _____

_____                _____

Alignment_____        Times Used_____

_____                _____

**30-30**    _____                _____

_____                _____

_____                _____

Alignment_____        Times Used_____

_____                _____

_____                _____

**30-10**    _____                _____

_____                _____

Alignment_____        Times Used_____

_____                _____

_____                _____

**10-Goal**  _____                _____

_____                _____

_____                _____

_____                _____

Figure 14-20

HASH MARK TENDENCY DEFENSIVE ALIGNMENT CHART

Opponent Scouted_____

| Left Hash | | Middle | | Right Hash | |
|---|---|---|---|---|---|
| Front | Secondary | Front | Secondary | Front | Secondary |
| | | | | | |
| | | | | | |
| | | | | | |
| | | | | | |
| | | | | | |
| | | | | | |
| | | | | | |
| | | | | | |
| | | | | | |
| | | | | | |
| | | | | | |
| | | | | | |
| | | | | | |
| | | | | | |
| | | | | | |
| | | | | | |
| | | | | | |
| | | | | | |
| | | | | | |
| | | | | | |
| | | | | | |
| | | | | | |
| | | | | | |

Figure 14-21

### ACCUMULATED DEFENSIVE CHART

Opponent Scouted_____

1. First downs vs. opponent's defense                    _____

2. First downs running vs. opponent's defense            _____

3. First down passing vs. opponent's defense             _____

4. Rushing yardage vs. opponent's defense                _____

5. Passing yardage vs. opponent's defense                _____

6. Total offense vs. opponent's defense                  _____

7. Passes completed vs. opponent's defense               _____

8. Passes intercepted by opponent's defense              _____

9. Fumbles recovered by opponent's defense               _____

10. Times goal line defense successful          _____of_____

11. Times short yardage defense successful      _____of_____

12. Number punts or kicks blocked                        _____

13. Average punt return yardage                          _____

### Figure 14-22

# 15

# HOW TO TRANSFER INFORMATION TO THE STAFF
## (Scouts)

AFTER the compiling process is completed and the Varsity Staff is ready, the Scouts should make their report on the upcoming opponents. (See Chapter 1 for specific ideas concerning the schedule for transferring the scout report to the Varsity Staff.)

### ANSWER "HOW?" "WHAT?" AND "WHERE?"

Of course, as has been stated earlier, the reason for scouting opponents is to determine "How Can We Win?" This information is broken into two categories, defense ("What Must We Stop?") and offense ("Where Can We Move It?"). The Scouts' main job is to answer these questions the best they can with the compiled information they have gathered while scouting the opponents.

### BE HONEST

As the Scouts give their report to the Varsity Staff, they should be very straightforward and very honest. There is no place in Scouts' reporting for beating around the bush or just telling Varsity Staff members what they want to hear. The information about the opponents should be delivered in a truthful manner, and all questions from Varsity Staff should be answered in the same way.

It is very important to be honest when making scout reports for many reasons, but especially for these two reasons: (1) honest reporting to the Varsity Staff will make for a much better game plan and, (2) honest reporting will always maintain the integrity of the Scouts with the Varsity Staff.

## DON'T GUESS

Another important trait the Scouts must develop is to tell it like it is (or was) and not to guess under any circumstances. The Varsity Staff wants detailed information about the opponents, and is likely to ask the Scouts some very involved questions about personnel, offense, defense or kicking game.

If this happens and the Scouts can answer the question(s) from their compiled information, they should do so. If they are not sure, they should never guess. It is much better to say, "I am not sure" and then try to get the answer later. This practice will prevent the Varsity Staff from chasing shadows in their game planning, and will maintain the Varsity Staff's trust in the Scouts and their reporting in the future.

## JUST THE FACTS

The Scouts should report their finds to the Varsity Staff in a concise manner, delivering only the facts about the opponents which are pertinent. Nothing of importance should be left out of the report, but it should not digress into frivolous discussions about material which will not help in defeating the opponents. (This fact should be kept in mind by the Varsity Staff also. Many times, "Remember when so-and-so did such-and-such," probably hurt game planning and may even have been responsible for some losses along the way. The entire staff should have bull sessions, but at the appropriate times.)

## MAKE RECOMMENDATIONS

Scouts should enter into staff discussions concerning the opponents any time they feel they have something helpful and concrete to add which may help the game plan. The Scouts have seen the opponents in person, usually more than once, and should have some good ideas which will aid the Varsity Staff. This habit should not be carried on until a Scout becomes a nuisance, but at the same time, many valuable ideas can be conveyed to the Varsity Staff at the right time and in the right situation.

## WRAP-UP

The important thing to remember in transferring compiled scouting information to the Varsity Staff is to do so in the best manner possible to try and help the Varsity Staff prepare a successful game plan versus the opponents. Finally, Scouts should be sure that their transfer of information to the Varsity Staff includes the answers to "How?" "What?" and "Where?"

# 16

# HOW TO PREPARE THE GAME PLAN
## (Staff)

AFTER the Varsity Staff has received the scout report on the upcoming opponents from the Scouting Crew, work on the game plan can begin.

## PUTTING IT ALL TOGETHER

If the staff has properly prepared throughout the year, the game plan should go smoothly. Actually, the game plan against a particular opponent should have begun immediately after the game with them the past season with the post-game analysis (this holds for continuing opponents). Then, the off-season pre-scouting process (when the opponent's file is completed), the pre-season updating and review of the opponent's file, followed by at least one (hopefully three) scoutings of the opponents, and finally, film viewing and the complete scout report should all make the game-planning process much simpler.

(This chapter is closely related to Chapters 1, 2, and 3 in that each of these other chapters is at least partially concerned with game planning. The reader should check back to these chapters for further information concerning game planning, particularly for scheduling suggestions and more specific ideas having to do with offensive and defensive planning.)

Many football staffs have the players come in the day after a game to view films of that game. Some staffs also have the players run through a quick loosening workout after viewing the film. If this is the case, the Varsity Staff can divide the supervision of these activities, and allow part of the staff to begin work early on game plan procedures. If the players do not come in, the entire staff can begin game-plan work early.

### Review and Evaluate

Before the actual game planning begins, the Varsity Staff should review all the material available on the upcoming opponents very closely. If film is available, further review and confirmation should be done by each member of the staff, paying particular attention to the portion of the opponent's game that each coach is responsible for.

As the reviewing process takes place, the staff members should begin to evaluate and form opinions concerning the capabilities of the opponents. Personnel, offensive and defensive maneuvers, the kicking game and any available tip-offs should be evaluated with regard to what part each element will play in game-plan preparation. This process should be carried out thoroughly, because the result of this evaluation is actually the foundation of the game plan upon which all the hopes and preparation of the staff and the team rest.

### Plan Positively but Never Overconfidently

One of the most important aspects of game planning is the attitude of the staff. Regardless of how good the opponents may be, the staff should, from the beginning, be very positive-minded and remain so throughout the game-planning process. Anything less than this attitude will, whether the staff realizes it or not, have an adverse effect on the game plan itself. As a coach I worked with a few years ago once said, "If I didn't think I had a chance to win, I would stay home and watch television."

And if the Varsity Staff has a defeatist attitude as they go into planning and preparation for a game, it runs throughout not only the staff, but is passed on to the players also, no matter how hard the staff tries to keep it inside. A less than positive attitude will also cause the Varsity Staff to plan poorly in many cases, often to the point of going away from its best "stuff" to something totally new and unfamiliar. (This type of thing works on occasion, but helps cause defeat in many more cases.) Remember this: There never would have been, nor would there ever be again an upset in football if all the teams which were supposed to lose gave up and laid down. The game-planning process is where the foundations of all "upsets" are laid. Plan positively!

By the same token, when playing an inferior opponent the staff should not plan any less diligently than for a strong opponent. Overconfidence spreads just as rapidly as a defeatist attitude, if not more so, from the staff to the players. In other words, consistency—the one thing coaches want most from their players—must be a trait exemplified by the staff in game planning from week to week if the program is to reach championship caliber.

## WHERE CAN WE MOVE IT?

As has been mentioned earlier, the Offensive Coordinator should keep the question, "Where Can We Move It?" on his mind continually as he and the other offensive coaches formulate the offensive game plan. The planning period for the offensive coaches should begin as early as possible on game plan day. If the Scouts have not finished the scout report when the offensive coaches are ready to begin, they can review the opponent's file and view film on the opponents if available and begin the evaluation process in this way.

If time allows, the Offensive Coordinator can speak briefly with the Scouts to see if the opponents used any new alignments or other defensive maneuvers the night before. He then can talk to the Head Coach and together they can go over the ideas that are beginning to form with respect to a tentative game plan. After the scout report has been given by the Scouting Crew, the offensive coaches can begin concrete work on the game plan.

Since each Offensive Coordinator is likely to attack each defensive alignment a little differently than the next, the following list of suggestions will be very general in nature. If followed at least to some degree, these items should help in offensive planning.

1. Plan open-mindedly.
2. Attack defensive weaknesses in 1, 2, 3 order.
3. Know in 1, 2, 3 order what you plan to use in each situation.
4. Explore all possibilities, then form a firm plan.
5. Make all your planning point toward answering "Where Can We Move It?"

Figure 16-1 provides a good offensive game plan form on which the Offensive Coordinator can list which plays are to be used in the various situations which will arise. Figure 16-2 shows a similar offensive game plan form for those who depend on a strong audible system for calling offensive plays.

## WHAT MUST WE STOP?

This question should be answered in every phase of the defensive coaches' game-planning sessions. If the Defensive Coordinator has time, he should have a quick word with the Scouting Crew to check for anything different the opponents may have done the night before. Then, until the Scouts finish the compilation process, the defensive coaches can review the available information on the opponents and evaluate them. It would be beneficial if the Defensive Coordinator and Head Coach could get together early to compare notes and express any ideas which may be forming as to a tentative game plan.

After the Scouts have presented their report, the defensive coaches should begin work on the defensive game plan in earnest. The defensive staff should keep the following things in mind as the game plan is being formulated:

1. Be open-minded in planning.
2. Know what has to be stopped in 1, 2, 3 order.
3. Decide the specific alignments, adjustments, stunts, coverages, etc., which will be used in certain situations.
4. Check out all possibilities, then develop a firm plan and stick with it. Figure 16-3 illustrates a defensive game plan form which may be used to determine alignments according to situations and field position.

## HOW CAN WE WIN?

While the offensive and defensive coaches are working on their portions of the game plan, the Head Coach (unless he is in one of the above groups) can be formulating his ideas about the overall game plan. Also, the coach or coaches responsible for the kicking game should be formulating the game plan in this area.

Once all the reviewing, film viewing, evaluating and preliminary planning is done, the Head Coach should meet with the offensive coaches to formulate the final offensive game plan. Likewise, he should meet with the defensive coaches and the coaches responsible for the phases of the kicking game to finalize the game plan in these areas.

There are so many things which must be done in a short time to prepare for game after game during the busy season. If the Head Coach has a chart such as the one shown in Fig. 16-4, he not only will have all of the game plan close at hand, but will also be able to fill in the other information and have all the pertinent information concerning the upcoming game close for ready reference at any time during the week.

## STAY WITH THE GAME PLAN

Another important aspect of game planning is that once the plan is formulated, the staff should stick by it very closely. It will be a good idea for the entire Varsity Staff to meet together after everything is finalized to clarify all provisions of the game plan for each coach. Once this is done, the game plan should be adhered to closely throughout the week, unless an unexpected injury to vital personnel forces a change. If the staff develops a habit of formulating a strong game plan and sticking with it from game to game, the team will naturally have more confidence in the game plan, in the staff and in themselves as a result.

## WRAP-UP

Proper game-planning procedures can best be wrapped up through the following suggestions as they apply to each staff's needs:

1. Pre-scout and pre-plan well (off-season and pre-season).
2. Scout thoroughly (and use the scout report in planning).
3. Plan open-mindedly and explore all possibilities.
4. Develop a firm, well-organized game plan.
5. Stick with the game plan (together).
6. Make sure to answer these questions wisely:
   (a) Where Can We Move it?
   (b) What Must We Stop?
   (c) How Can We Win?

OFFENSIVE GAME PLAN vs. _____

Down and Distance

| | 1 & 10 | 2 & 5+ | 2 & 4- | 3 & 4+ | 3 & 3- | 4 & 2+ | 4 & 1 |
|---|---|---|---|---|---|---|---|
| R U N N I N G   P L A Y S | | | | | | | |
| P A S S E S | | | | | | | |
| G O A L   L I N E | | | | | | | |
| T R I C K   &   S P E C I A L | | | | | | | |
| 2   M I N   D E L A Y | | | | | | | |

Figure 16-1

AUDIBLE OFFENSIVE GAME PLAN vs._____

| Opponent's Alignment | | Down and Play | | | |
|---|---|---|---|---|---|
| | | 1 | 2 | 3 | 4 |
| B A S I C | 1. | | | | |
| | 2. | | | | |
| | 3. | | | | |
| | 4. | | | | |
| V A R | 1. | | | | |
| | 2. | | | | |
| | 3. | | | | |
| | 4. | | | | |
| P R E V | 1. | | | | |
| | 2. | | | | |
| | 3. | | | | |
| | 4. | | | | |
| S H Y D G | 1. | | | | |
| | 2. | | | | |
| | 3. | | | | |
| | 4. | | | | |
| G O A L  L I N E | 1. | | | | |
| | 2. | | | | |
| | 3. | | | | |
| | 4. | | | | |
| L O N G  Y D G | 1. | | | | |
| | 2. | | | | |
| | 3. | | | | |
| | 4. | | | | |
| S P E C  P L A Y S | 1. | | | | |
| | 2. | | | | |
| | 3. | | | | |
| | 4. | | | | |

Figure 16-2

DEFENSIVE GAME PLAN vs._____

Down, Distance And Hash

| | 1 & 10 | 2 & 5+ | 2 & 4- | 3 & 4+ | 3 & 4- | 4 & 2+ | 4 & 1 |
|---|---|---|---|---|---|---|---|
| **L E F T  H A S H** | | | | | | | |
| **M I D D L E** | | | | | | | |
| **R I G H T  H A S H** | | | | | | | |
| **G O A L  L I N E** | | | | | | | |
| **L O N G  Y D G  &  P R E V E N T** | | | | | | | |

Figure 16-3

GAME PLAN vs._____

1. Officials confirmed _____  _____  _____  _____
2. Eating arrangements confirmed at_____for_____
3. Pre-game group meetings begin at _____
4. Pre-game warm up begins at_____

## Kicking Game

|  | K.O. | K.O. Return | Punt | Punt Return | Ex.Pt. | F.G. |
|---|---|---|---|---|---|---|
| 1. Substitutions | _____ | _____ | _____ | _____ | _____ | _____ |
|  | _____ | _____ | _____ | _____ | _____ | _____ |
| 2. Fakes,onsides | _____ | _____ | _____ | _____ | _____ | _____ |
| Special plays | _____ | _____ | _____ | _____ | _____ | _____ |
| 3. Kick Blocks | _____ | _____ | _____ | _____ | _____ | _____ |
| &spec.Align | _____ | _____ | _____ | _____ | _____ | _____ |

## Defense

| | | | | |
|---|---|---|---|---|
| 1. Opp's. best athletes & Pos. | _____ | _____ | _____ | _____ |
| 2. Opp's. weakest ath. & Pos. | _____ | _____ | _____ | _____ |
| 3. Must stop - run | _____ | _____ | _____ | _____ |
| 4. Must stop - pass | _____ | _____ | _____ | _____ |
| 5. Must stop - unusual | _____ | _____ | _____ | _____ |
| 6. Our basic alignments | _____ | _____ | _____ | _____ |
| 7. Our adjustments | _____ | _____ | _____ | _____ |
| 8. Our stunts | _____ | _____ | _____ | _____ |
| 9. Secondary coverages | _____ | _____ | _____ | _____ |
| 10. Short yardage alignment | _____ | _____ | _____ | _____ |
| 11. Goal Line alignment | _____ | _____ | _____ | _____ |
| 12. Prevent alignment | _____ | _____ | _____ | _____ |

|  | Regular | Sh.Ydg. | Goal line | Prevent |
|---|---|---|---|---|
| 13. Special subs. | _____ | _____ | _____ | _____ |
|  | _____ | _____ | _____ | _____ |
|  | _____ | _____ | _____ | _____ |
|  | _____ | _____ | _____ | _____ |

Figure 16-4

OFFENSE

1. Opp's. basic alignment and coverage _____ _____
2. Best athletes & position _____ _____ _____ _____
3. Weakest athlete & position _____ _____ _____ _____
4. Variations - front _____ _____ _____ _____
5. Variations - secondary _____ _____ _____ _____
6. Short yardage _____ _____ _____ _____
7. Goal line _____ _____ _____ _____
8. Prevent _____ _____ _____ _____
9. Our base plays _____ _____ _____ _____
   _____ _____ _____ _____
10. Our passing plays _____ _____ _____ _____
   _____ _____ _____ _____
11. Trick & special _____ _____ _____ _____
12. Goal line plays _____ _____ _____ _____
13. Two minute _____ _____ _____ _____
14. Delay _____ _____ _____ _____

|  | Regular | Special | Goal line | Two Minute |
|---|---|---|---|---|
| 15. Special subs | _____ | _____ | _____ | _____ |
|  | _____ | _____ | _____ | _____ |
|  | _____ | _____ | _____ | _____ |
|  | _____ | _____ | _____ | _____ |

Meetings

1. Pre-game notes _____ _____ _____ _____

2. Halftime notes _____ _____ _____ _____

Figure 16-4, con't.

# 17

# HOW TO TRANSFER INFORMATION TO THE TEAM
## (Staff and Scouts)

AFTER the game plan for the upcoming opponents is finalized, the process of transferring the scout report/game-plan information to the team should begin as soon as possible.

## GENERAL VISUAL TRANSFER

The culmination of the compilation process for the Scouts should be the preparation of large poster board charts for the bulletin board. Most staffs like to have a personnel poster with pictures of the starters pasted on in their basic offensive and defensive alignments. (These pictures might be available from game programs the Scouts have collected.) If player's pictures are not available, the normal symbols for offensive and defensive personnel can be used. Along with player's names, weights, classifications, and any other information desired can also be added. If there is one particularly outstanding player, he may be identified by use of a special color in making the poster.

Some staffs also like to have basic offensive and defensive alignment posters on the bulletin board, with smaller insets showing other formations, alignments and adjustments used by the opponents. In many cases when space allows, other posters showing the opponents' two or three best running plays and passes are also very helpful to display on the bulletin board. (This practice will keep the major aspects of the opponent's team in view as a ready reminder for the players as they enter and leave the athletic area throughout the week.)

The bulletin board method can be used as the first transfer of information. If the players come in for film viewing of the previous night's game, by the time they are ready to leave, the posters should be up on the bulletin board. It is also a good idea to place the players' grades for the night before on the same bulletin board. This will draw the players' attention to the area and will help begin the transition in thinking about the next opponents. If the players do not come in for film viewing, the posters should be in place for the players to check over when they arrive for workout on Monday.

## VERBAL TRANSFER

### The Scouts

If possible, even if only for a short time, it is helpful if the Scouts (or at least one of them) who have actually seen the opponents in action give an abbreviated verbal scout report. Time will limit the verbal report to the most basic of information, such as the personnel, most-used alignments, best maneuvers, snap count and anything outstanding or unusual.

Probably the most important phase of such a verbal report by the Scout(s) will be a short question-answer period. After the report, the players can ask any questions they have of the Scout(s). Having seen the opponents in person, the Scout(s) can probably answer such questions more readily than the Varsity Staff, particularly early in the week.

### The Staff

The Head Coach will, of course, have some general comments to make about the opponents before on-field preparation begins. He should cover any areas he believes necessary before the team breaks up into groups to gain more specific information about unit preparation. Each Head Coach will vary in the depth with which he will discuss the opponents, according to staff size and the actual coaching duties he must carry out.

When the team breaks down into its various units, the Assistant Staff Members will speak to their players in very specific terms concerning the scout report/game plan. Such sessions should be concise and to the point, transferring all the important material about the opponents thoroughly. (At the same time, the Assistant Coaches must be sure not to ramble or discuss anything irrelevant. If this happens, team members will pay less and less attention in these sessions as the season goes on, and time is too precious to waste in this manner.) These sessions are likely to be carried out in conjunction with the printed scout report/game plan which has been prepared for handout to the players and which will be discussed in the following section.

## SPECIFIC PRINTED TRANSFER

Probably one of the best methods a football staff can use in developing the game plan is preparing printed handouts of the scout report/game plan for the players. If all phases of the scouting and game-planning process were carried out to the letter, many more teams would probably be much more successful.

The important thing about preparing the scout report/ game plan handout for the players is making sure that all the vital information about the opponents is included in a concise, understandable fashion. Some of the items which will probably be included in the scout report portion of the handouts are

1. Offensive and defensive lineups and key replacements;
2. Formations and alignments used by opponents;
3. All basic offensive plays and defensive maneuvers;
4. Special plays or defensive actions;
5. Kicking game information.

The game-plan portion of the handout is likely to include

1. Offensive game plan versus opponent's projected defenses;
2. Line blocking and special offensive variations diagramed;

3. Defensive game plan (front and secondary) versus opponent's offense;
4. Different or special defensive manuevers diagramed;
5. Kicking game plans.

Another important item to remember in transferring the printed scout report/game-plan handouts to the players, is that the Varsity Staff should make sure this material is digested by the players. There may be reams of printed material and handouts coming to the players from other classes and from many other areas in their lives, and the scout report/game plan can sometimes get lost in the shuffle if not given a very special significance. Aside from thorough discussion of the scout report/game plan and strong encouragement from the staff for the players to study the reports, short tests can be given to the players once or twice a week on the printed material. This is an excellent form of encouragement for the players to keep up with the material and to assure the staff that the players will put in time studying the material. To be sure that the players keep up with the reports, take them up the last day of workout before the game.

## FILM

Of course, if current film is available on the opponents, it will be the best medium of showing the players exactly what the opponents are like, what they can do, and how they do it. Most of the vital information about the opponents will be revealed through film.

The staff may want to be judicious about what portions of film they want the players to see. This is especially true if the next opponents are not a particularly strong team or if a poor game is being viewed. It is a seemingly natural trait for players to anticipate that the opponents will play just as they appear on film. If the opponents come into the game mad or upset, this can be disastrous. The practice of showing the players all or only portions of films on opponents will, of course, be up to each staff in its own situation.

## WRAP-UP

The Varsity Staff, in transferring information about opponents to its players, should try to pass the information along in the most understandable and concise manner possible. The staff should also keep the following things in mind in transferring information to the team:

1. Be direct; do not waste time or effort on unimportant material. Get the vital information across.
2. Use every feasible method available to assure complete information transfer.
3. Be sure the players realize the importance of the material.
4. Use tests or some other form of encouragement to be sure the players are studying the information.

# 18

## HOW TO PREPARE EFFICIENT WORKOUT ORGANIZATION
### (Staff)

### MERGING THE GAME PLAN
### AND WORKOUT SCHEDULES

MERGING or combining the game plan with workout scheduling must be closely coordinated if the game plan is to be successful and yield the desired results. Four very important facets of the planning process were saved for discussion at this point because it is so vital that they be an integral part of workout organization. By following these four steps, the game plan/workout combination can be one and the same.

(1) The post-game evaluation should be scrutinized closely for the possibility of any necessary changes that must be made to improve one or more phases of the team's play before the next game. This facet of preparation will also include the results of the self-scouting process (if applicable) of the past game. Any outstanding tendencies which have been set in the last game and picked up by Scouts through self-scouting should be altered as part of the game plan and inserted into the workout organization.

(2) Review the film of the past game with the purposes of grading personnel and making any necessary changes in this area which will improve efficiency for the next game.

(3) Add any special offensive, defensive or kicking game maneuvers designed to take advantage of particular flaws in the opponent's game.

(4) Hold a Varsity Staff meeting for finalizing the game plan. Once the plan is agreed upon during the meeting, the staff should organize a tentative workout schedule for at least the first day's workout. The extent of the workout organization may well depend upon the amount of preparation time the staff has together before workout each day. If the entire staff does not have a period of time before daily workouts in which to plan, this meeting will be very important to the first day's workout organization. If the staff has a conference period before workout each day, the planning can be done at that time.

Whatever the scheduling and organization situation, it is most important that the above-mentioned facets, as well as all of the game plan, be strategically woven into the week's workouts through proper organization.

## GENERAL WORKOUT ORGANIZATION

As the staff begins tentative workout scheduling each week, here are several items it will be wise to consider with respect to the general aspects of proper workout organization.

1. Develop a sound game plan and stay with it. Nothing is so disconcerting to a football team than to have the game plan change throughout the week's workouts. If new maneuvers are part of the game plan, they should be tested very early, and those which are not usable should be thrown out after the first workout.

2. Film of the opponents should be used to illustrate a lifelike situation with regard to the opponent's personnel and maneuvers during workouts. While the team is viewing films of the opponents, the staff should point out particular mannerisms and maneuvers and then have the scout team personnel duplicate these actions specifically in workouts during the week. This practice can add a very important dimension to game preparation, and if handled correctly, can make the

scout team members take a tremendous amount of pride in
their helpfulness in preparing the regulars for the game.

3. Make all drills relevant to the game plan. Most staffs do an
excellent job of organizing each individual workout. In some
cases, however, there are two major flaws in workout organization. First, some staffs may only organize for organization's
sake, rather than for the purpose of carrying out the game
plan. Each opponent is different and must be prepared for a
little differently. Therefore, the workout scheduling and
organization should be flexible enough to differ from week to
week to properly prepare for each opponent. Do not let an
ironclad workout schedule become an obstacle for you.
Remember, do not organize the opponent into the workout
schedule; but organize the workout schedule around the
opponent and the game plan. Second, many coaches develop
habits of drilling and working out the same basic way week
after week, and therefore get into a rut. This is bad, particularly if it is done for the sake of certain drills, which may
be good, but have little relationship to preparing for each
specific opponent. This statement does not concern warm-up
activities, agility drills or individual ability-improvement
drills, but refers rather to the group, unit and team drills
which should all point in some way to preparing to defeat
the next opponent. Be flexible and do not drill for drilling's
sake, but drill to defeat the opponents.

4. Spend enough time on the kicking game. Workout organization should include a strong evaluation of the opponent's
kicking game in comparison with your own. Then, the
appropriate amount of time should be planned for this phase
of the game. Remember, many close games are won or lost
indirectly through the kicking game. For these reasons, be
sure to spend enough time on the kicking game in preparing
for each opponent.

5. Recognition is another important area which should be
considered in general workout organization. To be well
prepared and to promote confidence, the staff must include
enough time on this phase for the players to be able to
recognize quickly and correctly the opponent's alignments,
formations, maneuvers, personnel and replacements. Make
recognition time in workout an organizational priority.

There are, of course, many other areas in general workout
organization which will be considered by various staffs be-

cause of the different circumstances involved in each program. The above ideas are offered to spur the staff into examining its general workout organization to see if it is combining the game plan into each workout and if there are any areas presently being overlooked in the general planning process.

## SPECIFIC WORKOUT ORGANIZATION

There are so very many different factors involved in specific individual workout organization that there is no way to do justice to discussing the entire process here. I think there are three areas, however, which can be pointed out that will highlight workout efficiency, conserve time and improve implementation of the game plan through proper specific workout organization.

### Time Segmented Workouts

The practice of breaking down individual workouts into small time segments is almost universal among football coaches. Some use 15 minutes as the base time frame, some use 10 minutes and still others use 5-minute segments. I especially like the 5-minute segments because the workout can be divided into very small portions systematically and can be divided differently by each coach throughout individual and small group drills until it is time for unit and team drills.

Take, for example, the Secondary Coach, the Defensive Line Coach and the Linebacker Coach. Using 5-minute segments, and having different needs as to individual and group work time, and being allotted 30 minutes for both, their individual and group workout time may be divided as shown here:

| Secondary | Defensive Line |
|---|---|
| Individ.—2 periods (10 min.) | Individ.—3 periods (15 min.) |
| Group—4 periods (20 min.) | Group—3 periods (15 min.) |

Linebackers

Individ.—4 periods (20 min.)

Group—2 periods (10 min.)

Dividing the workout into 5-minute segments allows great flexibility in scheduling and still keeps the workout totally organized. In the 5-minute segmented workout, a student manager should keep time and at the beginning of each segment blow an air horn or whistle to signify the time to the Staff. Also, numbered, colored cards (about 11″ × 11″) should be used to signify the time segment change (from period 1 to period 2, etc.) each time the whistle or horn blows.

Dividing a two-hour workout into 5-minute periods will allow 24 such periods of work which can be either a highly organized workout for a full staff, or simply a well-planned workout for a limited staff. This type of segmented workout also makes it very simple to sequence the unit and team drills to fit the game-plan preparation activities.

Figures 18-1 and 18-2 show examples of workout forms which feature the 5-minute segmented workout.

### Sequenced Group, Unit and Team Drills

The 5-minute segmented workout is very conducive to the sequencing of full group, unit and team drills. The 5-minute segments provide a framework in which a specific number of actions or plays may be run if properly sequenced.

By sequencing, I mean the outlining on "hold-up" cards (used by the Coaches) of all the group, unit and team drills in a specific order and running these activities in the particular order in which they appear on the cards throughout the portions of the workout. Most staffs use this method to some degree, but it should be thoroughly planned out before each workout by the Coordinators or the Head Coach for maximum time-saving effect.

Sequencing can be done as follows: take the offensive portion of the workout, for example. The Offensive Coordinator lists in 1, 2, 3 order on a card all the offensive maneuvers he plans to work on in the workout. He then draws the opponent's defensive alignments and maneuvers that he wishes to work against on the hold-up flip cards and numbers each alignment. He then lists, by name and number on another card, in 1, 2, 3 order, each of the defensive alignments and manuevers that he wishes to work against in sequence. The coach who works with the scout team running the opponent's defense uses the defensive sequence card to run the defenses in order and holds up the flip cards in sequence to show each alignment as it is to be run against by a specific offensive maneuver.

This process eliminates talking the scout team through alignments and saves a great deal of time in which many more offensive maneuvers can be accomplished. The process is reversed for defensive workout and it should also be used in the kicking game and in group and unit drills. If not enough coaches are available for smaller group and unit work, a student manager or even a player can accomplish the sequence card and flip card process.

Sequencing a workout requires a little planning, but will yield approximately twice as many drills and maneuvers accomplished in the same amount of time as an unsequenced workout. Also, it is a very good method for organizing the game plan into each workout without leaving out important features.

## Make Team Drills Gamelike

Segmenting and sequencing workouts provide the staff an excellent opportunity to bring the game plan into proper focus in each workout by organizing the activities so that the same situations can be worked on before the actual situations occur on game day. Doing this is very important to the understanding of the game plan by the players and to the success of the game plan itself. This is especially true if the game plan is devised around tendencies, field position and hash placement.

The first thing to remember in organizing proper situational, gamelike workouts is to use the entire field and *not* to work out in one familiar spot all the time. (This is one serious problem which seems to become a habit with many staffs.) Use gamelike situations such as these.

1. Field position and hash placement (offense, defense and kicking game)
2. Goal line offense and defense from hash placement

3. Two-minute offense and prevent defense from field position and hash placement
4. Forcing bad plays defensively and working against making bad plays versus pressing alignments (live contact)
5. Working in crucial situations offensively and defensively (critical down and distance, etc.)
6. Special plays—making them offensively and stopping them defensively
7. The big play—making them offensively and stopping them defensively
8. The kicking game from all situations including field position and hash placement
9. Working on fumble and interception situations both offensively and defensively

If the staff will simulate real life situations into the workout, following the scout report/game plan, the team will do a much better job carrying out the game plan successfully on game day.

## WRAP-UP

If the staff organizes workouts with the game plan foremost in their minds, this will bring about more successful results, particularly if the workouts are scheduled by workable segments and sequenced to save time and simulate a more gamelike atmosphere. The more organized and situation-oriented a team's workouts are, the easier the game plan can be installed and the easier it will be understood by the players and, therefore, the better the results. Be sure to merge the game plan into workout organization properly and include all the proper ingredients in the scheduling of workouts and then carry out the workouts with a common purpose—to defeat the opponents.

VARSITY WORKOUT vs._____

| | MONDAY | | | TUESDAY |
|---|---|---|---|---|
| 2:35 – 2:55 | Defensive Meetings | | | |
| 2:55 – 3:15 | Offensive Meetings | | | |
| 3:15 – 3:25 | All players on the field for specialty | | | |
| 3:25 – | Cals. | 1 | | Cals. |
| | Offensive Workout | 2 | | Defensive Workout |
| | | 3 | | |
| | | 4 | | |
| | | 5 | | |
| | | 6 | | |
| | | 7 | | |
| | | 8 | | |
| | | 9 | | |
| | | 10 | | |
| | | 11 | | |
| Break | | 12 | Break | |
| | Defensive Workout | 13 | | Offensive Workout |
| | | 14 | | |
| | | 15 | | |
| | | 16 | | |
| | | 17 | | |
| | | 18 | | |
| | | 19 | | |
| | | 20 | | |
| | | 21 | | |
| | | 22 | | |
| | | 23 | | |
| | | 24 | | |
| | Conditioning | 25 | | Conditioning |
| | | 26 | | |
| Defensive Specialties | | | Offensive Specialties | |
| Weights for all other players | | | | |

Figure 18-1

VARSITY FOOTBALL PRACTICE SCHEDULE

DAY_____          DATE_____

              BEAT_____

        PREPRACTICE ROUTINE:              PRE-PRACTICE ROUTINE:
        DEFENSIVE PRACTICE                OFFENSIVE PRACTICE

1._____     1._____
2._____     2._____
3._____     3._____
4._____     4._____
5._____     5._____
6._____     6._____
7._____     7._____
8._____     8._____
9._____     9._____
10._____     10._____
11._____     11._____
12._____     12._____
13._____     13._____
14._____     14._____
15._____     15._____
16._____     16._____
17._____     17._____
18._____     18._____
19._____     19._____
20._____     20._____
21._____     21._____
22._____     22._____
23._____     23._____

SPECIAL NOTES TO SQUAD:

Figure 18-2

# 19

# HOW TO GATHER AND USE POST-GAME EVALUATION
## (Staff)

No coaching staff should miss the opportunity of evaluating each game they play for the purpose of future planning, both during the current season and for the next season. Through the use of three processes—game statistics, game film and self scouting—self-evaluation can be accomplished rather simply.

## EVALUATING THE GAME

After each game, the Varsity Staff should write up a brief report on the game. This report should include information on the success of the scout report and game plan, mentioning any changes or suggestions for improving these procedures for the next season. Also, new or different formations, alignments and maneuvers used by the opponents should be noted. Finally, all the vital statistics for the game should be recorded for evaluation.

### Statistics Evaluation

During each game, the team statistician or an assistant coach should keep statistics on the offense, defense and kicking game for later evaluation purposes. (In limited staff situations, a student manager or teacher may keep the stats, or they can be gathered to a lesser degree from newspaper accounts of the game.) Figure 19-1 on page 216 illustrates a post-game evaluation statistics chart which, when completed, will yield most of the vital statistics for a game.

From this chart, several evaluations can be made. Among these are

1. The success of the scout report/game plan;
2. Offensive output (broken down into categories);
3. Kicking game averages;
4. Defensive success;
5. Changes which should be made to improve effectiveness before next game (include in game plan).

## Film Evaluation

The film of the past game should be evaluated and personnel graded as soon as it is available to the Varsity Staff. (Some full staffs have the assistant coaches, who are often the Crew which scouted the team played, grade the film.) This allows the Varsity Staff to evaluate the film from a team standpoint and get on with the game plan for the next opponent. It also allows the Scouting Crew to evaluate its scouting job on the opponents and to make changes or corrections in procedures, if necessary, before scouting again.

Film evaluation gives the Varsity Staff the opportunity to further evaluate (above and beyond the post-game stat chart) these items first-hand:

1. The game plan;
2. Offensive, defensive and kicking game successes and failures;
3. The opponent's offense, defense and kicking game (for next season);
4. How particular formations, alignments and maneuvers worked;
5. How special plays and defenses worked;
6. Personnel (very important for the game plan for next opponents);
7. Opponents' returning personnel (for next season);
8. Any changes in strategy before next game.

## Self-Scouting Evaluation

Having your team scouted by your own scouts is an excellent way to evaluate the past game from several standpoints. Self-scouting can be done by an entire Scouting Crew from a fully staffed program, or it can be done by one coach on a medium staff, or it can be done by a student manager or knowledgeable teacher on a limited staff. Regardless, the self-scouting process is worth whatever it takes to have it done.

Self-scouting is most helpful in finding out which, if any, tendencies or tip-offs your team may be setting or exhibiting. Knowing these idiosyncracies before playing again is most helpful and can even be the difference between winning and losing. Making changes to eliminate tendencies and tip-offs as part of game planning can completely throw an opponent off track and have a big part in a successful game plan.

## USING THE EVALUATION IN PLANNING

The Varsity Staff should be sure to use the various forms of post-game evaluation to its advantage in planning for the next opponent. Through the use of the post-game stat chart (Figure 19-1), game film and self-scouting, the staff will normally find at least a few areas which can be changed or improved, and when added to the scout report/game plan, should make the team stronger for the next game.

## AN EARLY BEGINNING FOR NEXT SEASON

After all post-game evaluation has been concluded and the game plan for the next opponent is finalized, the Varsity Staff should see that all information used for the past opponent (including post-game evaluation material) is filed in the opponent's file. If this is done immediately after the opponent is played, and the material is evaluated, it will give the Varsity Staff and the Scouts a head start when off-season pre-scouting begins later. (And it assures that none of the important material will be lost or misplaced.)

Following are the materials which should be placed in the opponent's file at this time:

1. Scout report;
2. Formation, alignment and play posters;
3. Game plan;
4. Post-game statistics evaluation chart;
5. Film (if not to be used again);
6. Self-scouting information.

## WRAP-UP

Post-game evaluation is a very important phase of successful coaching which is often overlooked, at least in part, by many staffs. The Varsity Staff would be wise to do as much as possible in this area, for it may well mean the difference in one or more games this season—and next season.

### POST-GAME EVALUATION STATISTICS CHART

*Offense*

1. First downs     _____
2. Rushing yardage     _____
3. Passing yardage     _____
4. Total offense     _____
5. Total offensive plays     _____
6. Number passing plays     _____
7. Number running plays     _____
8. Avg. gain per down     _____
9. Avg. gain per down (run)     _____
10. Avg. gain per down (pass)     _____
11. Number of times stopped for loss or no gain     _____

*Kicking Game*

1. Avg. punt distance     _____
2. Avg. punt return distance     _____
3. Avg. kickoff return     _____
4. Opponents avg. kickoff return point     _____
5. Blocked kicks _____ by opponents _____     _____

Figure 19-1

*Defense*

1. Opponent's first downs
2. Opponent's avg. gain per play
3. Opponent's avg. gain per run
4. Opponent's avg. gain per pass
5. Opponent's number of plays
6. Opponent's number running plays
7. Opponent's number passes
8. Opponent's pass completions
9. Our fumble recoveries
10. Our pass interceptions
11. Number of times stopped on G.L. or short yardage

Figure 19-1 (cont'd.)

## CAPSULE

Coaches should remember that this scouting/game-plan guide is meant to be used just for that purpose—as a guide. It will not be possible for every staff to use all the information contained in this book. This guide was written to be an aid to the staff in preparing and organizing its scouting and game-planning procedures, and to provide some proven ideas, techniques and information for improving this part of the football program where needed.

### Other Points of Interest to Remember

1. Webster's Dictionary describes a *Scout* in this way: "A person sent to spy out the enemy's strength, actions, etc." (A Scout should think of his work in this way, using a spirit of adventure to help him seek out ways to defeat the friendly "enemy" on the football field.)
2. Webster's also describes a *Plan* as: "A scheme for doing something; an outline worked out beforehand." (The Varsity Staff should use the scout report and all other available information to develop a scheme for defeating each opponent, and outline this scheme in detail—beforehand.)
3. Excellence in Scouting and Game Planning is essential for a consistently successful football program.

# INDEX

# Football Coach's Complete
# SCOUTING and
# GAME-PLAN GUIDE
## Bobby Rexrode

Now you can go into every game with a virtual 13-point advantage, because this book provides you with a well-organized scouting system that insures your team maximum pre-game preparation.

By effectively scouting your opponents, your team can handle all the multiple offenses and defenses prevalent in football today. And by using the scouting system described in this guide, you can get and use the specific information you need to overcome the sophisticated offensive maneuvers of multiple motion and shifting, as well as defensive stunting, slanting and offsetting.

This complete scouting system incorporates the same three-part scouting strategy Rexrode himself has used to lead his teams to 13 championships!

## PART I—PREPARING THE GAME PLAN

A well-organized game plan is essential to successful performance . . . and since game-plan preparation is the single most important responsibility of the Head Coach, he should have a systematic method which will eliminate speculation and guesswork. In this book, you discover the nine essential elements of a successful game plan. You also get sample schedules for game-planning sessions and workouts . . . as well as new, more effective techniques for using game films and statistics in developing the game plan.

## PART II—SCOUTING THE OFFENSE

The Defensive Coordinator needs to know what the opponent's offense is doing. He should always be aware of what must be stopped. Rexrode shows you nine specific areas to plot when reading the opposing offense. He then shows you how to draft specific defensive game-plan maneuvers based on the opposing offense.